"In running, as in life, a companion shortens the road. Though 3,000 miles of ocean separate us, I have found Jim Frawley, via his podcast parables, the consummate running companion: encouraging, empathetic and, glory be, funny. To his enormous credit, he always observes the unspoken rule of the great coach—bring the slowest guy home. After 40 years building businesses and bolstering community, I have grown deaf to most business gurus but Frawley: his views I do care about because I know he cares."

—Máirtín Ó Muilleoir, former Finance Minister of Northern Ireland and former Lord Mayor of Belfast.

"Success in the new economy is reserved for those who take responsibility for their actions, treat others with respect, and can stand on their own two feet. In order to find your place, you have to start with a focus on what you can control: yourself. Jim's book provides a framework to get you started."

—Joe Moglia, former Chairman, TD Ameritrade; Chairman of Athletics, Coastal Carolina University.

"With so much change happening in nearly every aspect of life, having an approach to change management is more important than ever. And taking control of our personal situations is the first step. Jim shares the questions you should be asking to empower yourself to take the first step"

—Paula Polito, Global Financial Services Executive

"Accessible and practical, yet authoritative. . . . *Adapting in Motion* presents a powerful combination of the human spirit with business acumen that provides readers with a useful blueprint for navigating and striving during times of change— which is every day. A must read!"

—Terrence E. Maltbia, Associate Professor of Practice & Faculty Director, Columbia Coaching Certification Program (3CP)

"Working in city government is not for the weak of heart—it is a true test of spirit. In this rapidly changing world, public servants and other leaders must be able to adapt and remain relevant as we work to address the ever-evolving needs and priorities of those we serve. Jim understands and shows that while it may not be easy to adjust to change, we are each capable of doing so; and in order to make our mark, we must."

—Kathryn Ott Lovell, Commissioner, Philadelphia Parks and Recreation

"Jim has a knack for tackling the complicated issue of change management, drawing upon his dynamic career spanning numerous industries and economic cycles and interdisciplinary approach to problem-solving. Jim's trademark down-to-earth manner and his authentic approach have made him popular as an executive coach. In his book, he draws on his experiences to connect with the audience and his insights will certainly help professionals develop timeless strategies to successfully withstand and manage changes of every scale."

—Claire Simier, Managing Principal,
Simier Partners

"While getting ahead can initially be easy, it is ultimately the most difficult, and necessary, to put in the hard work. However, it's something no one can take away from you. In *Adapting in Motion*, Jim brings his uncanny sense of 'know how,' humor, and true grit to inspire and direct professionals to open the curtain to their true potential."

—Larry Black, CEO, Tulle New York

ADAPTING IN MOTION

FINDING YOUR PLACE IN THE NEW ECONOMY

Jim Frawley

JONES MEDIA PUBLISHING

Printed in the United States of America

ISBN: 978-1-948382-06-9 paperback
JMP2020.3

DEDICATION

For Gabby, who has believed in me since day one and makes me want to be the best I can be.

It is the last thing left in me, and the best: the ultimate discovery at which I have arrived, the starting-point for a fresh development. It has come to me right out of myself, so I know that it has come at the proper time. It could not have come before, nor later. Had any one told me of it, I would have rejected it. Had it been brought to me, I would have refused it. As I found it, I want to keep it. I must do so. It is the one thing that has in it the elements of life, of a new life, Vita Nuova for me. Of all things it is the strangest. One cannot acquire it, except by surrendering everything that one has. It is only when one has lost all things, that one knows that one possesses it.

—Oscar Wilde, De Profundis

CONTENTS

AUTHOR'S PREFACE   1

ACKNOWLEDGMENTS   3

INTRODUCTION   7

PART ONE: BE AWARE   23

    CHAPTER 1: RECOGNIZE CHANGE   23

    CHAPTER 2: BE AWARE OF WHAT'S
    HAPPENING   31

    CHAPTER 3: SOCIETAL CHANGE   41

    CHAPTER 4: WORKPLACE CHANGE   49

    CHAPTER 5: CONSUMER AND PSYCHOLOGICAL
    CHANGE   63

CHAPTER 6: BE AWARE OF YOUR ROLE AND
ABILITY TO RESPOND   71

PART TWO: BE PREPARED   83

CHAPTER 7: PREPARE TO PREPARE   83

CHAPTER 8: PHYSICAL PREPARATION   95

CHAPTER 9: MENTAL PREPARATION   117

CHAPTER 10: SOCIAL PREPARATION   141

CHAPTER 11: FINANCIAL PREPARATION   159

PART THREE: BE TEACHABLE   165

CHAPTER 12: LEARNING PAINS   165

CHAPTER 13: PUT HUMILITY IN ITS PLACE   171

CHAPTER 14: BE CURIOUS   183

CHAPTER 15: EMBRACE VULNERABILITY   191

PART FOUR: BE WISE   197

REFERENCES   209

ABOUT THE AUTHOR   215

AUTHOR'S PREFACE

A note from Jim:

Writing a book is a process; writing a book like this is catharsis.

What you're going to read in the following pages are the lessons I taught myself, through trial and mostly error. Sometimes I wish I had focused on or learned these things earlier in life, but on reflection I recognize that I wasn't ready to hear them.

It was the process of self-discovery that led me to become an executive coach for CEOs, businesses, teams, and entrepreneurs. I work with these fantastic people to help them manage and adapt to change in their own way, and I love what I do.

One of the best lessons I've learned in all my work is that we can't make a change or adapt to change unless we're ready and willing. Our own realizations will have to open the window to a new world and a new way of being. It's uncomfortable, but totally worth it.

Those realizations are what we strive for. They say that it's impossible to experience happiness if you're always seeking it. But that's too black and white. The seeking is the happiness, and what you learn along the way becomes your satisfaction. I've learned to be a learner, and it's the best lesson I could have received. This book is one way to share what I'm now aware of.

Thanks for reading. I hope you enjoy it.

Jim

ACKNOWLEDGMENTS

Everyone should write an acknowledgements page—it brings out all kinds of great feelings

Acknowledgements have to start with my wife: This book would never have happened without her. She inspired it, patiently read it, gave comments, and listened to my whining while I did it. You're a legit superhero—thanks for making me and my world better.

I also want to thank Isabelle for making me question everything about myself to make sure it's what I want to teach the next generation. You'll teach me more than I can ever teach you.

Thanks to Mom, Dad, Maureen, Jeanne, Christine, Mike, and Kevin, for helping forge me through the fire, through warmth and love, and keeping me honest. Who needs a village when your family is an army?

Thanks Pierre, Joanne, Pop, Pete, and Melissa for being my second family and making me feel welcome. I recognize how lucky I am to have in-laws that I love and respect and whose company I enjoy.

Susan, Lowell, Sara, and the rest of the Ithaca-area crew for sharing with us the place to think and be creative; it's one of my favorite regenerative places to visit and where the outline of this book was finalized. We love you guys.

Thanks Jones Media Publishing and the crew that held me accountable to finally getting this book done.

And, finally and in absolutely zero particular order: Joe Moglia, Dr. Terrence Maltbia, Dr. Rachel Ciporen, Lowell Garner, Tony Hacking, Paul Allen, Greg and Emily Roache, Claire Simier, Frank Seminara, Máirtín Ó Muilleoir, Audrey Wallace, Jim Hausmann, Kieran Fagan, Catherine Norris, Robert Burton, Jimmy Hawkins, Pat Sheldon, George Sinnott, Christine Glancey, Rick Pitino, Paula DeLaurentis, Sean O'Dowd,

Larry Black, Emily Ruiter, Mac Coyne, Tanayha McLeod, Tim Coyne, Matt Foley, Mike Greenly, Jorge Tejeda, Alan Goldstein, Paula Polito, Denis Wuestman, Rachel Rubinstein, Bob Dorsey, Josh Foreso, Abe Puerto, Angela Macropoulos, Dennis Wayland, Dan Miller, Nick Malito, Daryl Lloyd, Anthony Ferrier, Pat McGeehan, Sean McNeill, Paul Welykoridko, Tony Lyons, and the lady working at the Newark United lounge who told me I was "walking my purpose"—you are each a testament to how a small, seemingly insignificant comment to me can have an outsized impact. All of you hold a spot (and probably don't know why) in my "learning and positivity document," and I use it for inspiration on the daily.

INTRODUCTION

History admits no rules; only outcomes.

—David Mitchell, *Cloud Atlas*

Many of us wish we knew what the future held—it would make everything so much easier. Having a roadmap for our planning would alleviate so much uncertainty and stress if we just knew what "the right decision" was.

As humans, we're generally terrible at preparing for the future because we prepare according to past experience. This presents a challenge because what built our experience, that old world, is now gone. Our old way of preparing is gone. The world you knew growing up is long gone, and the world of today is on the conveyor belt to history. The world you'll see in five years will be starkly different from today in ways that we can't even describe or imagine.

Will we survive this change? Of course, but it won't be easy to deal with. Change will be forced upon us faster than we can adapt. It's why businesses and individuals hire me as a coach: to help them adapt to change. This is a book to help with that transition.

The good news is that we *are* adaptable. Like a chameleon, we can change our colors. There is a way to prepare for change when you don't know what change is coming. The preparation is internal and requires much introspection, work, and development. It takes a learning mindset, or something that I call a *cathartic vulnerability*; that peaceful feeling you get when you recognize that things outside of your control aren't your responsibility. It takes giving up things you've always had and learning to like some other new things in their place. It requires a social network: solid, in-person relationships with actual humans with whom you speak and share emotions and feelings. It takes you being you and putting your best foot forward. Preparing for change is a journey that never ends—but for me it's been the most fun journey I've ever been on.

The start of my journey was the morning of my epiphany, when I awoke literally and figuratively. As the sun rose, rays of light coming through the window and the Statue of Liberty in the distance, I woke up with an absolute sense of calm. My body had a slight tingle; I sensed serenity. The world was silent and still, but not noiseless. Something felt different, but I couldn't figure it out.

This calm was unusual, and it slowly dawned on me why. Most mornings I either had a slight headache from the beer garden downstairs or a pit in my stomach from the dread of going to the office. Neither were there. Laying on my back and staring at the ceiling, I also realized that my apartment had a different smell: the fragrance of my grandmother's beach house emanated throughout, despite my apartment being in the shadow of New York City. I felt my grandmother's presence, despite her passing a few years earlier.

I'm not particularly religious and I don't use drugs, so all this should have felt fairly disconcerting to me. Yet I felt energized and refreshed. Thoughts, beliefs, and stress I was struggling with melted away. My shoulders and neck had no tension for the first time in what felt like ages. It was like I had drawn a line in the sand and turning thirty had pulled me across it.

The date was April 28, 2009—my thirtieth birthday. (I'll pause here for you to do the mental arithmetic gymnastics to see where your age is in relation to mine). Some might say thirty is a milestone, but for me it was more. It was the morning my epiphany woke me up and showed me the secret to my life.

This wasn't just a wake-up-feeling-refreshed, the-sun-is-shining, thirty-doesn't-feel-so-bad type of emotion. It was a straight up—no bullshit—shock to the mind and system that had me lying in bed and thinking for the better part of the morning, despite it being a work day.

There are a few definitions of *epiphany*—some religious, some scientific, some neither. A simple definition is that an epiphany is a sudden, supernatural realization or understanding, an absolute revelation, an insight into something that you've never realized or that could be contrary to everything you believed before. In some cases, an epiphany is a sense of awakening—and light and sunshine and lasers and beauty and flowers and overwhelming. I don't use the term lightly.

An epiphany is also highly personal and individual. It comes when you're alone, for you alone. It's based on your worldview, your personality, your history, your experiences, and more. An epiphany for me could be a complete non-event for you.

With that said, I have never been the same person since that day.

I think about that morning often and wonder about the causes. Perhaps a distant ancestor was sending messages from another world, or maybe the wine I drank the night before was fermented with some wicked good shit.

In reality, it was a mental act of desperation. My mind accumulating so many challenges, regrets, fears, and thoughts over time that it exploded into a message: "Wake up, asshole, this is what you are too stupid to realize."

I can't tell you exactly what my epiphany was about because an epiphany generally can't be expressed in words, so it wouldn't make sense if I tried. In essence, though, I experienced a plethora of sensations and emotions before I got out of bed. I realized that I wasn't spending my time in the way I wanted to or with the right people. My priorities completely aligned in a freaking instant. Like flipping a switch and light flooding a room, everything clicked.

This realization brings me to the part that does matter. Since that day, I've been on an upward trajectory of learning and personal development that's quite different than my previous path. You'll read about my "before," the stress, relationships, and work that left me empty and dry. Much of my story will relate to you, and what I've learned may be very relevant to you as we all continue to deal with change.

Prior to my magic morning, I was an archetype: late twenties, living in the Northeast, working for a financial firm off Wall Street. There were, and continue to be, thousands just like me: grunting through inconsequential work, resenting their office and commute, hiding their depression and sadness, flirting with vices like alcoholism, and often wondering why we aren't pursuing our "purpose" (or some other nonspecific, arbitrary, fulfilling desire).

The renaissance I experienced fundamentally changed the way I live. Because my perspective changed, my behaviors, thoughts, and actions changed. I credit the epiphany with starting a chain reaction of events that continue to make my life more satisfactory and enriching. Since that day, I met the woman who would become my wife and started a family, I changed careers, I launched a business, I quit drinking and smoking, and I completed a triathlon. My days are better; I sleep better. I still have challenges, but they're easier to tackle and I handle them in a better way. I wouldn't change anything.

Yet those statements leave a lot out. In order to understand my change, you need to understand me. In this book, I'll share how my late twenties were a time of abject sadness and loneliness, despite financial success and appearing happy. I'll share how my behaviors destroyed relationships and how I alienated myself from people I cared about. And without having close personal relationships, I was eaten alive on the inside by bottled up anger, resentment, and depression. I manipulated people to get things I wanted; my closest relationships ended up being centered around a pub. On reflection, my epiphany was the greatest thing to happen to me; it helped me to realize not only was I responsible for all of that but it was also my responsibility to change it. My thirties were a journey of development, providing clarity and a sense of being that continues today.

"That's nice, Jim. Stories of change are a dime a dozen." Correct. Yet we love reading them. And the reason we love reading them are twofold. First, we love to see the difficulties that other people have so that we can feel superior. And second, we want to see a redemption story to relate it to our personal situation.

And this is where my story relates to you:

We're right smack in the middle of unprecedented change. We can each sense a massive, unseen mountain ahead of us, one that will challenge us physically, psychologically, and spiritually—an enormous macro-transformation across all facets of life, which will change the way we operate. This shift is coming faster than we can control and is already incredibly uncomfortable.

It's so uncomfortable because the change is ongoing and unending. There's no predictable future to which we can anchor ourselves. So we float, one day at a time, with that uncertain feeling in the back of our minds. The only way to survive and respond is to take a step back and focus on micro-you. And focusing on micro-you takes nuance, skill, and support; it takes a perspective that I'll share throughout these pages.

The changes are as broad as how we operate as a society and as small as how you get cookie recipes on your smartphone. But more importantly, change impacts our way of life from a business and career perspective, and that's where my focus will lie. More than ever, a person and their company have to be in lockstep in order to be successful. A company will survive the change only if its people are ready to adapt. And that takes investment by both the company and the individual.

I won't say this is a self-help book. There are plenty of those out there, telling you what to do and what to think. I would never presume to do that. Again, your worldview and experiences are different than mine, and you need different things than I do. But, then again, any book is a coloring book if you have a crayon, and any book is a self-help book if you learn something from it.

So, this book, like all books, *is* designed to help. It's designed to help you navigate through the misery that is your work. It's designed to help you articulate that uncertain feeling you get that comes as you pull into the office. It may be the tonic that fixes the pit you feel in your stomach when the alarm goes off at 6:00 a.m. and you stare at the ceiling, slowly feeling your shoulders tense as you think about the report that's due and how much of a pain in the ass Andy from Accounting is.

This book will also help you beyond the office: It's not just for people who hate their job. It's about facing the difficult questions we have ignored for years. It's about navigating that fascinating jungle known as your mind and figuring out the person you wish to be. It's about taking steps to realize what you are dreaming about accomplishing but never have. Your results may vary. But I knew something was changing when my daydream started to change—it went from just "Oh, man. I could just give all this up and go volunteer in Africa" to "What would it take to start this business?"

Your timing couldn't be better. As the economy and workplace change, those who don't give themselves permission to evolve and change their thinking will be left behind. Organizations are doing it in droves—to stay relevant, they're investing in new technologies and marketing strategies to reach new people. They're (hopefully) investing in their employees to learn new skill sets, and if they aren't doing that, then they're looking for new people.

In exactly the same way, *you* have to invest in you. As job roles get eliminated and businesses disappear, your skills will need to evolve and your "psychological capital" will need to deepen.

To be crystal clear: you, the reader, are the sole person responsible for being in a position of success as the economy changes. This book will drive your accountability. While I'm of the belief and opinion that organizations have an *absolute* obligation to support their people and get them prepared to respond to change, you're responsible for how you use that platform.

Thanks to technology, work and life are inextricably linked now. We're constantly tuned in; we check emails on weekends, and our jobs are a significant part of our identity. As lifespans get longer, making that part of our identity something that aligns with who we want to be is vital. Who we want to be takes discovery.

We all have *innate abilities*: characteristics and skills that appear to be part of our core. Some are with us since birth, others are developed over time and just become a part of who we are. One of my innate abilities is the ability to jump from smaller, micro-thinking (the trees) to broader, macro-thinking (the forest) and back. I'm particularly adept at identifying the things that *could* go wrong and preparing for them. It's a big reason my coaching business is successful, and it's a big reason my clients hire me.

Often, we're so focused on our little microworld that we miss the bigger picture. We go on carrying out our daily routine, and the world changes around us, leaving us unprepared to respond. Or, we're so focused on the change and the big picture that we can't focus on the daily steps needed to respond. My epiphany merged these two views.

In responding to any big change, I tend to bring my clients on an arc. And while this didn't crystallize for me right away, after reflecting on my journey, I realized that I followed a new logic, a new way to deal with uncertainty. As such, there are four steps to responding to significant change:

1. Be Aware
2. Be Prepared
3. Be Teachable and Learn
4. Be Wise and Execute

This arc has been quite successful for my clients and is a phenomenal framework to outline the big changes, while leaving space for us to fill in micro-tactics to respond as we try to find our place in the new economy,

This book is designed to be used as you see fit. I'm big on setting goals and making progress. I've learned many (sometimes harsh) lessons over time, and I've attempted to put them into a framework that other people may find beneficial. I'll do my best to avoid bullshit ambiguous statements like "Just be happy" or "Find your purpose," because statements like that really don't mean anything, and they don't help you change.

What I'll provide are a series of questions and reasons why I think you should answer them so that you can figure out what would make *you* happy and satisfied and purposeful. You'll learn how to move from desire to action. The work has to be your own, and identifying what really matters and what's important to you is what creates that

North Star to guide you through turmoil, volatility, and difficulty.

I've taken training, education, research, and experiences and co-opted it into something that's tangible. This book is the result of that. This book can be a reminder, a portable workshop, or a coaster for your coffee. But I must caution you before you read this book: if you don't address yourself and if you don't prepare for the significant, uncomfortable, volatile change that is knocking at your door, then you do so at your own peril. I can't stress it enough.

The technological revolution, adaptation, and new reality are all part of a train coming right for us. We can sit and stick our head in the sand, kicking the can down the road and waiting until it's too late to respond, or we can hit it head on. Those who do the work now—who prepare and lay the foundation to adapt to change—will be light years ahead of those who wait for it to happen. For you fans of Aesop, this is truly an ant and the grasshopper story (unlike the ant, the grasshopper failed to prepare for the winter).

It's about cultivating a cautionary view, but a view designed to inject confidence into your decision-making abilities. People who can see change before others heed it are incredibly valuable, to both organizations and communities.

In his book *Principles*, Ray Dalio tells a story about when he presented European leaders with some challenging forecasts regarding their economy around the time of the 2008 financial crisis. Ray is the founder of Bridgewater Associates, one of the largest and most successful hedge funds in the world. In the book, he says, "Just as U.S. policymakers had before 2008, the Europeans did not fear what they hadn't experienced before. Because things were good at the time and the picture I was painting was worse than anything they'd experienced in their lifetimes, they found what I was saying implausible" (Dalio 2017, 102). We can remember how Europe, and the rest of the world fared.

Yes, we all can feel that things are changing. But to be aware of specific change, and how it impacts you, is the first step in understanding what it is we're dealing with. So, with that, let's begin.

PART ONE: BE AWARE

The lawn cutter might just as well not have been there at all; the gardener will be there a lifetime.

> —Ray Bradbury, *Fahrenheit 451*

CHAPTER 1: RECOGNIZE CHANGE

In 1999, a movie came out called ***Blast from the Past***. I've watched it a few times—and for some reason it sticks with me. I love it. Christopher Walken, Sissy Spacek, Brendan Fraser, and Alicia Silverstone.

Great cast. Fun story. Feels good. It's certainly not a groundbreaking film, but for me it accomplishes what I think all movies strive to do—it entertains. I'm only slightly embarrassed to admit it's one of my favorites.

Here's the plot in a nutshell: a guy mistakes a series of events, believing a nuclear attack is imminent, and he takes his family down to a fallout shelter where they end up staying for thirty-five years. He then sends his now thirty-five-year-old son up to the world to see what has become of civilization. Needless to say, there was no nuclear war, life went on, and now Brendan Fraser is walking around 1990s USA with a 1960s mindset. He meets a lady, falls in love, yadda. Adorable.

Is the movie ridiculous? Of course. Original? Sure. Entertaining? You bet.

The story is intensely relevant to today. Brendan Fraser entered a world that initially looked like it went through a nuclear fallout (Los Angeles in the '90s was a rough place). But the more he walked around, it eerily felt the same as the world his father described. The people looked the same, wearing somewhat similar clothes; storefronts and food looked the same; and he was able to communicate using the same language.

While similarities existed, 1990s LA was very different from 1960s LA. Technology, habits, social progress, subtleties of language, infrastructure, and transportation—all of these changed over time. He was stunned to see both television and the mail carrier were "in color." You could feel the uncomfortableness through the screen when he innocently used language that was commonplace three decades before (like referring to a mail carrier as "a negro").

The movie made light of the changes between thirty-five years, but that type of gap is significant. That significance is forgotten when the never-ending day in, day out obscures all of the changes, and then when we pause to look, a lifetime goes by. If you want to recognize how much change can happen in a lifetime, know that Anne Frank, Martin Luther King, and Barbara Walters were all born in the same year. I find it extraordinary to think through not just the major events of the twentieth century that each of them represent but also the mindset that has shifted in the past hundred years.

We're adaptable people when we have the time to adapt. And the amount of change that we're going to be experiencing, while it will be a challenge, isn't the challenge that we should be focused on. Instead, it's the *speed* of change happening faster than we can adapt—that's the bigger problem. What changed in thirty-five years now takes only two to three.

So, let's understand change so that we can move out of paralysis, or simple observation, and start on our journey of awareness.

Change is slick. It creeps up on us in small and big ways, often at the same time. It surprises us; we adjust and adapt, and we move forward. For example, you're trying to lose weight, and each day you weigh yourself, you see minimal progress, but you stay committed. However, one day you step on the scale, and *bang*: you realize that you lost twenty pounds. In the moment, you don't realize the incremental change that has happened. You don't feel each fat molecule drip off your gut as it happens, yet the incremental shedding leads to something big.

But what happens when the surprising change is too much for us to adapt to or handle? What happens when a series of changes occur and society gets torn apart? We need to be focused on that change.

Much has been made of technological advancement and of how society is growing. Some fear that robots, algorithms, artificial intelligence, and the like will destroy the world, while others think it will lead to a utopia where there's no work, we can sit around drinking wine and learning how to paint. The answer will be somewhere in the middle.

But "somewhere in the middle" isn't good enough. We want to plan and prepare. A very human challenge is that we always want to know the answer. We want to make predictions, have them come true, sit back, be comfortable, and have the world align to our expectations. Like everything else, we're making predictions on where technology will bring us, when in actuality we really have no idea. No matter our theory on where change will take us, reality will always pick a different path.

Knowing reality takes a different path shouldn't preclude us from planning, however. There's significant value in planning. The simple act of thinking through a situation provides insights into alternative solutions and allows you to be ready to act.

Regardless of what life throws our way, when we properly prepare, we're light-years ahead of others who didn't plan at all. If you've ever tried to plan something, you know it rarely goes according to plan. Think through any serious conversation you've had: sharing your feelings with someone, speaking to a boss about a raise, breaking up with someone. In your head, it was a simple, rehearsed conversation from beginning to end. In reality, you didn't get through your speech, and they didn't respond the way you expected.

Preparing for those conversations gives you clarity, however. While the conversation with your boss may not go as you expect, you still, in your mind, have an expectation on a result—for example, a raise of a certain amount. By being aware of your surroundings, your worth, your expectations, and your reactions, you're in a strategically better position.

The first step in planning for change, therefore, is awareness: awareness of what is happening and awareness of how we can respond. That's it.

The conversation regarding technological or societal changes very typically jumps to our future roles and statuses. We fill the gaps of what we don't know with our own emotional responses and fears of the unknown. But it's a jump too far, too soon. Let's start with an awareness of what is happening today to each of us. Then we can begin to talk about how we can respond.

Chapter 2: Be Aware of What's Happening

Primarily driven by technology, the world is changing faster than we can adapt, and we know that change is very uncomfortable. That uncomfortable feeling will grow in the coming years. We know this because of two factors: the law of accelerating returns and something called VUCA (don't worry, I explain).

The law of accelerating returns is the brainchild of Ray Kurzweil, a futurist and technology expert, often speaking on change and where technology is taking us. In his book *The Age of Spiritual Machines*, Kurzweil (1999) discusses how certain fields, such as technology, tend to grow exponentially over time. When things grow exponentially, they can become unwieldy.

It makes sense. The larger the item, the bigger the change. A small forest fire can be quickly contained, but over time, it gets to be more of a challenge. A campfire that gets out of control can be stopped with a bit of water. If one hundred acres of forest are burning, that will quickly double, and you have a major change of landscape coming.

It follows, in similar fashion, the work of R. Buckminster Fuller (1982), who proposed that knowledge (or change, for that matter) can double in a half-life. What took one hundred years to get from point A to point B only takes fifty years to do it again, then twenty-five years, and so on.

As an example, think about the massive amounts of change in knowledge and innovation that happened in the twentieth century. In 1900, we barely had cars on the road. What blows my mind is that plastic, radio broadcasting, and tea bags were all invented *after* 1900.

Fast forward one hundred years. Musically, LPs came and went; 8-tracks, cassettes, CDs all rose and died in that amount of time to the iPod. We have vacuum cleaners and Tickle Me Elmo. We had evolved to rely so much on technology that there was a massive fear of world collapse with Y2K. World change skyrocketed.

That's quite the jump. Now to think of the first twenty years of the twenty-first century, we've *already* made a bigger jump. Cell phones have morphed into video chat and bandwidth has increased; we created the first bioengineered synthetic cell; Tickle Me Elmo still exists. Moving beyond, we have autonomous cars, algorithms are making job roles obsolete, and the fundamental way that we live and interact is being upended, from Amazon logistics to artificially created limbs.

When you think about what you were doing in the 1990s, think about how amazing it was that you could chat on a dial-up modem; then, fast forward to today where you can order anything in the world and have it in your possession in a day—it boggles the mind. It feels amazing. It feels like excellent progress.

And much of it *has* been excellent progress. Technology is responsible for incredible growth in all kinds of areas: medically, we're saving so many more lives; socially, I attribute much of the growing human equality to technology; and communicatively, the increase of available information around the world has shown that people of different races, religions, and orientations are just that: *people*—fellow humans with emotions and feelings that we experience ourselves. Technology has helped remove a veil of ignorance and uncertainty about other people.

The other side, however, is a bit more challenging because we can't see it, only feel it. Our attention is effectively gone. Technology is being used to change and manipulate behavior. Our ability to focus is at an all-time low. Our attention is for sale, with corporations and apps fighting for our limited spans through beeps, dings, and vibrations.

For the first time, Facebook has been named in divorce proceedings. Psychologists and neuroscientists are doing studies and publishing books on why children can't focus enough to read a full book. Depression, anxiety, and stress levels are at all-time highs. The technology that is progressing us so well on a macro, society level is also hurting us at a micro, individual level. The technology that was supposed to help us not work—and sit around and paint—is leaving us with the feeling we have less time than ever. And even if we ever did get to just sit around and paint, would our minds be still enough to enjoy it?

As we go about our lives, and change continues to happen, it will get harder to keep up. Compounding change, doubling our rate of change tomorrow, will be overwhelming. The larger the item, the bigger the change. Thinking through the amazing things happening today, and progress we're making, we can't begin to imagine the change that's going to happen in just a decade.

We can't imagine it because the jump is too big. It's not like we can see the next step. The compounding change is a jump, a leap into a direction that we can't visualize or determine. We have to just go with the flow, which isn't nice to hear because when we plan for things, we like to know what we are planning for.

I didn't promise there wouldn't be math, so here's a quick example of compounding change. If I gave you $1 on the first day of a month, and asked you to spend it, you would have no problem. And if I promised to double that amount each day, with the caveat that you had to spend all of it that day, you would probably agree. So, on the second day, you would receive $2, on the third day $4, and on the fourth day $8. All of these amounts are small and easy to spend.

Here is where it gets interesting. By just the fifteenth day, you would get $16,384 to spend. By the twenty-first day, you're getting over $1,000,000 and by the end of the month, you're looking at more than half a billion dollars a day. The acceleration quickly becomes unwieldy after that point.

Day	Compounding change with dollars
1	$1
15	$16,384
30	$536,870,912
50	$562,949,953,421,312
100	$633,825,300,114,115,000,000,000,000,000

Describing it as *amazing* doesn't do it justice. If you stand on the fifteenth of the month and get your $16,384 and look ahead to the week, it would be difficult to imagine getting over $1,000,000 at the end of it. And after a month, you can't even comprehend the number at day 100 (that is over $633 octillion).

Today's number, whatever it is, is going to be significantly larger tomorrow. We just don't know how large because we use the past to predict our future. Can you even visualize $633 octillion? Do you even know what it means? In fact, pause for a moment, and go back to day fifty. Can you even visualize $563 trillion? We don't have the real mindset capacity to appreciate this kind of growth and scale.

When we think of the past twenty, thirty, or forty years, we remember a different world, and we have diverse memories of the past. Not only were technology or services different (I used a typewriter growing up) but our perspective growing up was very different as well. Watching technology advance as a child without responsibility was fascinating and fun; however, watching it advance at the same speed as the parent of a teenager is very different. Seven-year-old me had a very different view of 1986 Bronx than my parents. Same Bronx, same Chaffee Avenue house, different perspective. With age comes different responsibilities and viewpoints, all influenced by the uncomfortable adaptation necessary in constant-changing times.

In the table above, using the past to think of the next set is a mistake. As you sit on Day 15, thinking of how to spend that $16,384, it won't be relevant on Day 30 or 50—the challenge is on a completely different level. The change we've already experienced will be compounded to points where we can't imagine. For the same reason, we can't imagine what the world will look like in a decade or more.

It's exciting to think about but unnerving at the same time. Possibilities are endless but can be uncomfortable. We can draw on our experiences, but what do we do when they're irrelevant to the change we're facing, even when that change is happening today? And what happens when we get older, and it becomes even harder to keep up?

Which leads us to the next part: VUCA, which stands for volatility, uncertainty, complexity, and ambiguity. VUCA is based on leadership theories in the 1980s to articulate the challenges of responding to change. If you've worked in an office, you've probably heard of it, because companies and managers love to use acronyms that make them sound intelligent.

VUCA's popularity had a major resurgence during the 2009 recession. The economic challenges of that time period have shaped a generation. Volatility in the stock market paired with job prospect uncertainty, a complex mortgage problem, and an unclear future created a permanent psychological impact in the population. Even those who kept their jobs throughout the crisis reported significant stress increases simply because they didn't know if they would have a job the next day.

The reason VUCA had a resurgence is the same reason we need to talk about it today: change. The uncertainty of what was coming next led to stress, fear, and nervousness. As we'll see in the four types of change I outline below, each one has the potential to upend our belief systems, our expectations, and our self-worth.

There are four types of change I'm going to cover in part 1: societal, workplace, and consumer and psychological change. People write books on each of these individually, so it's a lot to cover, but my purpose is straightforward: I want to give an overview and understanding of where your focus should be, and these four types of change are going to have the biggest effect on you as an individual.

CHAPTER 3: SOCIETAL CHANGE

The easiest changes to see and account for are those happening across society. With the ability for everyone to share their experiences at the tap of a button, awareness and equality have made tremendous progress. Society, norms, and what's acceptable are constantly evolving.

It's important to recognize good change when it happens. I find it fascinating that there are people alive today who can remember when people weren't allowed to vote because of the color of their skin. In more recent times, I have personally witnessed sexual orientation discrimination, a challenge that has made much progress in recent years. A long, overdue shift has occurred on the value that women bring to the office and how pay and promotion levels should reflect that. All this is excellent progress, with more to be done and seen.

These are important steps. Not that we would need the research to justify it, but studies show that diversity, inclusion, and social justice progress is not just good for society but for business, the economy, and our personal mindset. Companies with diverse boards and leadership have higher profits; economic investment in underprivileged areas tend to have higher returns on investment. In his book *Social*, Matthew Lieberman (2013, 75) shares research showing that simply *seeing* people being treated fairly triggers the reward center in our brains. Fairness makes us think that we're eating chocolate. And chocolate is delicious.

But as with any progress, there are negative sides as well. Change is disruptive to status quo, which can drive a fear of the unknown. When we're unsure of what's happening, we feel control slipping away and we create false belief systems while holding on to negative stereotypes. We put down and attack things outside our world to feel superior to them and to regain control. Our natural inclination is to "slip into the negative" when our grass doesn't feel as green as the other side.

There are unwritten contracts that we all feel. As part of our experiences, we come to expect certain things, and we acquire a belief that we're entitled to something because of where we are at that particular moment. When you take a look at the growth, success, and productivity of the US economy since the Second World War, the American Dream has been alive and well, and many people throughout this country have come to expect that success to continue.

What we forget, however, is that the growth and productivity of the twentieth century wasn't normal or typical. It was an extremely odd outlier of normal economic growth. Because of several factors (e.g., global priorities, world wars, trade promises), America was fortunate to be in a position of success. That arc and timeline is beginning to come to an end, and that change and fear of the unknown can lead to turmoil. As we'll find out, the problem with unwritten contracts is that they can be rewritten.

In **Hillbilly Elegy**, J.D. Vance (2016) writes of his upbringing in the Appalachian Valley, where he describes his background, family, and experiences of growing up in an economically depressed area.

The book is a fascinating read into the psychology of America and about what happens when we grow up with social expectations that aren't met.

Like in many parts of America, the Appalachian Valley is hurting. Children aren't guaranteed a better life than their parents. After decades of incredible growth, factories and mines have closed, leaving people to look externally for individuals or organizations to blame for their problems and misfortune.

There are values in Appalachia that are commendable: loyalty, love of country, support of neighbors. But regarding society, there's a common self-defeating mindset among the residents. Vance shares stories of people who got jobs but never showed up because they thought they were better than the work. There's a mentality of "I deserve this, so I shouldn't have to work for it." The book is full of lessons, and most importantly, there's a discussion of the cross section between personal responsibility and general economic malaise.

It's partly a philosophical challenge, partly a psychological challenge. On the one hand, "Pull yourself up by your bootstraps" doesn't mean jack if there's no economy to speak of. On the other hand, if you sit and wait for someone to fix your own situation, it won't get fixed.

On the seesaw of individual accountability and economic fairness, we're now seeing individuals in depressed communities shift their ire outward to others. And it's understandable: it's easy and feels good. We don't want to swallow the hard pill of being "not good enough." When I have an expectation that something will be waiting for me, it's easier to blame you when it doesn't come to fruition than look at my own situation and see what I can do to change it.

In watching the conversation for the middle of the country, from Appalachia to Iowa to Arkansas, much of the discussion is about going "back to the way it was." People want the unwritten promise: the contract that promises them they can have what they expect. And the reason why is because white, middle-class America wasn't at the bottom of the food chain, and they now have a vision of how swiftly they may fall. The world has evolved, yet many haven't taken the steps needed to avoid being left behind.

People don't discuss what they need to do to make themselves more relevant in the new economy.

There's no discussion on creating new, different opportunities and learning new skills. Learning new skills is difficult work—many of us don't want to do that.

This gap has led to civil unrest and will lead to more as people direct their anger toward different groups of people (i.e., people different than them), whether socioeconomic, racial, or otherwise. The irony is that blaming others makes it worse for people already heading on the way down— it creates a chasm and distances them from the people on the way up.

While my book won't change the mindset of an entire country, there's a lesson you can learn in it. Yes, focusing on your accountability and competency as an individual and what you can control, will get you through the change. But awareness of the fact that you were promised nothing, are guaranteed nothing, and will receive nothing without working for it is a harsh plate to eat. It may not feel good, but it's just a fact of life, and it's not anybody's fault.

We need to fundamentally understand societal change and look at the macro view and how it impacts us individually, especially now as we look at the changing workplace.

Chapter 4: Workplace Change

As society shifts, so does the workplace. The evolving needs of a society will drive what businesses can and should provide. The changing marketplace, paired with advancements in technology, are upending the workplace in countless ways.

There are two points to make before talking about workplace changes. First, our work is part of our identity. It's highly emotional. Most people, if you ask them to describe themselves, will include their job in the description. Even retired people, when you ask them about themselves, will respond "an engineer" or "a teacher" or "an accountant," even if they haven't worked in a decade.

We spend most of our waking hours thinking about work. When ideas or projects are put down at the office, we take it personally. Our neighbors and communities are generally driven by our types of work because we live near people in similar socioeconomic situations. Work is a big deal and important for our psychology, our purpose, and our pocketbooks.

Second, it pains me to say, is that the sole purpose of a business is to make money. In the grand scheme of most business decisions, you're irrelevant. Granted, some organizations are better than others at how they treat their people, but at the end of the day, profitability comes before people, because if there's no profitability, then there will be no people.

We like to think that companies exist for their people or their customers, like so many of those ridiculous corporate slogans and ideals announce. But, in reality, focusing on products, employees, or customers is just a way of driving profit. Yes, much research shows that treating employees well is better for the bottom line, but we must remember that one doesn't preclude the other. They don't have to be tied together, despite what we wish to think.

Therefore, a juxtaposition exists. Despite investing our hopes, dreams, time, energy, and more into our work, the company we work for is pressured to and working hard to increase profit margins. Yes, some companies sacrifice some profit for other reasons, but as a person who has sat in the room while these decisions are discussed, any sacrifice in profit is aligned to a positive outcome down the line.

Now, a discussion should be had on what an appropriate profit margin should be, and the merits and limits of free market capitalism versus other isms, but I'm not going to solve that here. The answer is different for each industry and each company within it. There are those who like to make blanket statements about industry and expect everyone to fall in, but stating that all organizations need to operate according to your individual principles doesn't hold water. Everyone is the greatest parent in the world when they're complaining about someone else's kid.

I have my opinions on how much money is enough money, and what appropriate profits and loss would be. When I look at the sacrifice many people make for their company, I'd like to believe that there should be a significant slice of the pie shared back to them. And, when we look at the changes coming to the workplace, I would argue that organizations currently have an *even larger* obligation to their employees—in terms of not just money but also psychological capital and new skills—to get them prepared for the new economy.

I predicate my work with many of my clients on a company's obligation to its employees. In fact, many organizations are investing countless dollars on technology and processes that will eliminate overhead, increase productivity, and improve the bottom line. All of that sounds great. But what about the people?

A few years ago, I was brought in to lead an off-site conference for the human-resources group of a large healthcare organization. It was a two-day meeting, with business updates from different areas and intense discussions on what was "next" for the organization. It was all very interesting to see how the organization was thinking years into the future.

One of the presentations made my jaw drop. A person gave an overview of the technology that they were looking to roll out "to support the HR department." It showed that, through this system and analytics, future employees would be discovered, interviewed, hired, and have their offices set up without ever having to speak to a person at the firm. The cost of hiring new people would go down. The amount of time for onboarding a new person would go down. It was all a "win-win"; everyone cheered it and were very excited about the prospect.

The technology wasn't what made my jaw drop, as cool as it was. As I looked around the room, I saw people in the recruiting, onboarding, compensation, and business partner departments, and I could tell that none of them were thinking about how this was going to upend their jobs. Over sixty people were in the room; this technology would wipe out a quarter of them, and for the rest, it would fundamentally change how they work.

What disturbed me, as I reflected on it, was that there was no discussion, in any of the meetings for the ongoing human-resources strategy, on what the organization was going to do to prepare their people for this change. And we only heard about tech in the HR department—we didn't even cover tech changes in finance, legal, sales, or marketing. Where was the plan for the people who were going to be eliminated or for people who needed to reposition themselves?

I sent a note to the head of HR the next day, thanking her for inviting me to the meeting and outlining my commitments and next steps. I then posed the "people" question, asking if that would be covered at the next offsite. The question wasn't well received.

As an organization, they didn't feel it was their responsibility to take care of people who wouldn't be working at the company. They were certainly aware that there would be some "difficult discussions," and that they were looking at the expense a change in headcount would cost. In essence, the only conversation about people was how expensive it would be to pay for outplacement services. To say I was disappointed is an understatement.

But a lesson was learned, and it's something we all secretly know. Our growth and ability to be employed is ultimately our responsibility. To survive change, we need to make investments in ourselves to stay relevant. The smart people in that room on that day were thinking of ways to make themselves invaluable to the organization beyond their particular role. After all, roles are fairly arbitrary and likely to change.

Focusing on whether your job will be taken or changed is focusing on something you can't control. The question you should be posing is, How can you remain relevant as the changes come along?

That is a very different question with a potentially very different answer.

Jobs will be out there. The question will be whether you'll have one that you want. We're in an age where things happen so quickly at the office that adaptation and reinvention are now skill sets that we need to acquire.

The pressure to perform, and our timelines to succeed, are changing as well. I work with many senior executives who take on new roles and only have one or two quarters to make a significant difference. They're expected to change a culture and drive a profit almost overnight— which is difficult to do when the world around the office is changing faster than the company can adapt.

Because I understand how roles, responsibilities, and culture are changing so quickly, I like to tackle the problem from two viewpoints: the enterprise and the individual.

Let's start with the first viewpoint: the enterprise. The old workplace is gone. How the office functions is shifting, and the larger the organization, the harder it is to keep up. Society, demand, clients, and employees have all changed. In some instances, employees are working remotely, while others have people working in open-seating floor plans—a misguided attempt to drive collaboration. The office will continue to evolve with interesting experiments in response to operational changes.

But outside of changing real estate, the real challenge for organizations is the speed of change from a strategic point of view: (1) new initiatives are generally outdated before they can be implemented and (2) economic uncertainty leads to strategic stalemates.

A perfect example can be found in a Tennessee electrical company. Every five years, the Tennessee Valley Authority does an assessment on what demand it will need to account for over the next twenty years. It's a very important assessment, since the work needed to meet increased demand is expensive and takes a long time to implement. The study is an intensive process that takes them three years to finish and costs millions.

In a recent study, however, the company hit a snag. The industry is changing so quickly, and electrical demand has stalled so abruptly, that its last plan was outdated in less than three years. The company paid its millions and conducted the study, and when it was finished, the twenty-year plan lasted less than three (Roberts 2018). Essentially, the study's findings were outdated before it was even done.

Obviously, when a public utility deals with these challenges, it has major implications for society at large, but for a private or public corporation, it leads to a stalemate on making strategic decisions.

Let's talk about a past client, who I'll call Bob. Bob was the president of a new, tech-oriented division in a large financial firm. He was tasked with building up what would be a core component of the future of the larger organization. Since he was new in the role, and the board had high opinions and expectations of him, they thought it prudent to hire a coach to help with the transition. We worked on leadership and presence, the culture he wanted to drive and how he wanted to structure his team (standard stuff for a person in his situation). One of the big topics we often discussed was the strategic direction he wanted his division to take.

He had difficulty putting together his strategic vision because of the uncertain future. He felt that there were major forks in the road where he needed to make a decision today, and his decisions would have downstream impacts on the company many years down the road. His hesitation was understandable: because of his desire to be successful, he didn't want to make any wrong decisions. But by not making any decisions, the world would pass him by. It was a tough spot to be in.

Through coaching, we did several exercises to articulate the vision and culture he wanted to create and how his vision would align his group with the larger parent company. He discovered that the decisions he wasn't making were actually inconsequential. It didn't matter which decision he made—what mattered was that he made one. We got him to the point where he was able to move past the roadblock and make decisions, and the firm lined up behind him. But the stalemate caused months of indecision, indecision that had many potential consequences on hiring, investing, and potentially losing ground to competition.

The simple threat of change is preventing people from making the necessary decisions to help their organizations succeed. Companies are now faced with developing a new way to help individuals manage change at the office. They want simple, sustainable change-management programs, but they don't exist. They don't exist because in responding to macro change, we need to focus on micro thinking.

Which brings us to the second viewpoint: the individual at the office.

In addition to the challenges in how we operate, the individuals of the office, those agents driving the change, are having a helluva time as well. It's not just those strategic-planning programs and stalemates that are shifting, our day-to-day is now unstable. And people don't like a lack of stability, otherwise known as change.

For as long as ever, there has been big money in change-management programs: bring in consultants, they look at the change that's happening or is desired, and they put together a huge-ass deck with charts and numbers and pictures to tell management how to get the employees behind it. Management feels good because they think they learned something and consultants feel good because their presentation was over a hundred pages long. At the end of the day, nothing changes because it's a square-organization peg into a consultant's round hole. Nice work if you can get it.

Nothing changes because change-management programs don't work. They don't work because they're either focused on tactical changes when the vision of the end isn't clear, or try to force change on an unwilling population. To drive a change-management program without a clear vision is like potty training your kid without patience. It won't go well.

Change-management programs, or change-adaptation programs as I like to call them, need to have flexibility to be successful. And flexibility means giving up control and handing autonomy over to the employees. If you don't want your employees to have autonomy, then you need better employees. A McKinsey study estimated that 70 percent of change programs at work fail to achieve their goals, in large part due to employee resistance (Tams 2018). And I expect that number will increase.

Employees resist because the fear of the unknown drives stress, which is the biggest burden today for people navigating change. Stress doesn't just come from the office—it comes from uncertainty. And uncertainty drives negative behavior. And now we're back at VUCA. We don't like being told what to do—we want to do what we want and make our own rules because it feels more comfortable.

You can see the implications. Employees uncertain of their future are distracted, edgy, and less productive, which then bleeds into life outside of work. Combine this with the challenge of getting things done, archaic processes, and strategic stalemate, then the workplace quickly becomes unrecognizable.

What is concerning is that the workplace, for generations, has provided more than just monetary value to society. We don't just work for a paycheck; we also get status, structure, and social interaction. There's easily a link to be made between a breakdown of the traditional workplace and an increase in mental health challenges in society.

There's a study that comes out annually called The Masculinity Report: a survey of American men designed to "identify their values, priorities and factors which contribute to their emotional, physical, and mental health and well-being" (Barry 2018).

The first report was released in 2018 and had a fascinating finding regarding an American man's positive mindset. Far and away, above family and health, was job satisfaction. It's the number one driver of mental well-being for men across the country. Pair that with statistics that show that the largest suicide rate is in men over age sixty-five (i.e., when they retire) (National Institute of Mental Health 2017), or with the massive amounts of studies regarding women's mental health and the workplace, and you can see the power that work has over our well-being and our general lives.

We have lives beyond work, as we know, and we receive stress from change in other areas as well. Now, let's address the lovely, never-ending and always obnoxious marketing intrusions we constantly receive that affect our personal lives.

Chapter 5: Consumer and Psychological Change

We can't talk about evolving technology and a new economy without talking about how marketing and consumer behavior is evolving before our very eyes.

In the movie **Won't You Be My Neighbor?**, Fred Rogers (2018) discusses his motivations for creating the television show **Mister Roger's Neighborhood**: "In this country, a child is appreciated for what he will be: he will be a great consumer someday. The quicker we can get him to go out and buy, the better we are." Treating children as consumers, rather than children, was one of the things he wanted to change with his show.

In his book *Hooked*, Nir Eyal (2013) rose eyebrows when he outlined the psychology behind building habit-forming and addictive products. Primarily used by technology companies, he outlined the general process of how to get someone "hooked" on your product. (Lauded by some as a perfect textbook to create a new product and bashed by others on the morality of creating addictive technology, Eyal then went on to write another book on how to not be distracted by technology.)

The way we're being marketed to and sold to is a case study in taking advantage of buyers when they don't know what's happening. Social media (Facebook, Twitter, Instagram), phone applications (*Candy Crush*, *Farmville*, *Angry Birds*), and even news websites are all tapping into a similar formula to exploit a reward center in your brain. Companies create an addictive response mechanism for their product to drive more revenue through advertising.

The implications are astounding, and the entire playing field is changing. The consumer world used to be based on the worth or value of a product, but now it's a question of how much consumers are willing to pay. Airlines don't charge a set price for their seat: what you pay for your seat could be influenced by the type of phone you have, previous ads you have clicked, and other habits you have. By creating a profile on the type of spender you are, you could end up paying more for your seat than the person next to you.

And it's not just airlines. It's the same with "unlimited" mobile data plans (apparently, unlimited means having limits now), restaurant menus, and shopping sites like Amazon. In many instances, prices are charged based on the individual looking at it, not on what something is actually worth in the typical, supply-and-demand or profit-margin sense.

It puts a new spin on the warning "Buyer Beware." As a buyer, the responsibility to beware is, ultimately, on us. We shouldn't just assume that something works at face value; we should be digging deeper and thinking things through on what value that vintage Mr. T doll has for me.

Besides, with the ever-increasing amount of information out there, we rely on algorithms and technology to filter it for us. How can we guarantee the filter will operate in our best interest? And who is to say it should? Why wouldn't the algorithm work in the best interest of the company that created it?

On the back end of these marketing and consumer practices is data. There are massive amounts of money to be made in data points—those seemingly innocuous bits of information that most people don't care about. But how those harmless, innocent bits of information are compiled and used can end up negatively impacting you.

Most people I speak with are resigned to the fact that their information is taken, packaged, and sold. After all, they say, "I have nothing to hide." But what if this information could be used against you? I know a real estate agent who won't speak with her clients inside of a house because of the assumption that there are hidden cameras and microphones to give the sellers an edge based on the decisions the buyers are making.

What if your tracked eating habits end up causing you to be denied health coverage? Your driving habits triple your car insurance? Could you be denied a job because of behaviors at home? We often think of what we gain from this data collection, but we haven't yet seen what can be denied us as well.

People can make their own decisions regarding their data, the positives, and dangers (I won't take a side on it). Some enterprising individuals have gone all in and give people the opportunity to sell their data directly. A cafe in Rhode Island doesn't use cash, but allows you to pay your tab by providing data about yourself (Schaffel 2018). It's a whole new way to operate.

The fact remains that we are constantly targeted and sold to. Studies show we see **over ten thousand brand messages a day**. This does two things: (1) it influences our decisions over time and (2) it drives psychological stress. Which brings us to psychological change.

All of these changes, by themselves, are big. But when you take a step back and look across all of them, it can be intimidating. Feeling a lack of control, constantly being marketed to, having our focus hijacked like a commodity leads to psychological distress. Always being "on" and having our belief systems frequently uprooted leaves its mark. In our efforts to manage and adapt to change, it feels as if we don't even have the ability to slow down enough to even determine or evolve our belief system.

Much is being written and researched on the link between mental health deterioration and loss of privacy. Gabriel García Márquez once said that "all human beings have three lives: public, private, and secret" (Martin 2010). What damage can occur from losing any level of privacy or secrecy? I would argue that everyone has at least one thing that they don't want anyone else to know. I could probably fill a garage with mine.

Though causality is difficult to establish, research is now linking increases in anxiety and depression to the loss of privacy and the rise of social media. Constantly selling yourself and always being "on" is stacking an additional layer of stress onto an already stressful life. I've always found it fascinating and upsetting that so many people need massive amounts of medication just to get through their daily lives. We're starting to understand why.

The Centers for Disease Control and Prevention reports that in the first fourteen years of this century, antidepressant use in the United States increased 65 percent; also, more than one in eight individuals above the age of twelve are taking antidepressants regularly, and a quarter of these people have been taking them for over a decade (Pratt, Brody, and Gu 2017).

There are plenty of reasons, and we can blame many things. Some research focuses on social media and privacy and other research shows that a lack of meaningful, in-person social interaction is the culprit. Some argue it's that people have lost a sense of purpose, and I've heard others posit that the negative news driven by a twenty-four-hour news cycle has wedged into your psyche.

All of these, I would argue, have merit. They each make sense and pass the smell test. Each person is different, and each of the above causes could influence someone differently. And how people are influenced could be driven by background, gender, race, sexual orientation, education, and more.

It's not enough to remind people that we have a choice in how we respond. Yes, we can choose the apps we use or the websites we frequent. But we're in a mode of information overload that can't be merely fixed by disconnecting. In 2011, Martin Hilbert and Priscila Lopez estimated that enough information was shared through technology for each person in the world to receive 174 newspapers a day In 2020, The International Data Corporation

(IDC) estimated that we were creating more than *thirty times* that amount (over 5,000 newspapers per person, per day) and that by 2025 it will be almost *100 times* that amount (over 16,000 newspapers per person, per day). That's exhausting. And a lot of information to filter.

"The quality of your life is determined by the quality of your inner dialogue" is a quote often attributed to the American philosopher Frederic Hudson. Understanding what's happening externally and keeping an eye on change is important. But driving your internal conversation is what will get you past the change; therefore, the nature of your inner dialogue determines how you live your life.

And that, my friend, is an excellent segue into an awareness of how we can respond to change.

Chapter 6: Be Aware of Your Role and Ability to Respond

In 2019, I competed in an Ironman triathlon race. I had always thought something like that was both out of reach and certifiably insane, but as I approached my fortieth birthday, I decided to give it a shot in a midlife crisis sort of way.

In an Ironman, you complete a 2.4-mile (3.86 km) swim, followed by a 112-mile (180.25 km) bike ride, followed by a 26.2 mile (42.20 km) run (otherwise known as a marathon). Yes, you do them one after the other on the same day within a certain amount of time. Yes, it takes a long time (longer if you're me), and yes, I'm happy I did it.

For many people it's a life-changing event. It takes full commitment, from your diet to your training schedule. It's an incredible testament to what your physical body can accomplish, but I would argue it's a greater testament to what your mind can handle. An Ironman race is a physical activity, but it's a mental sport.

One of the weird dichotomies of triathlons is that it feels like a team sport while also being a solo event. There's an amazing community, filled with supportive and understanding people, but you—and you alone—have to do the work and finish the race. And when you're on a course for ten, twelve, fourteen, or even sixteen hours, the mountain of being a solo event makes itself apparent.

In preparing for my race, I swam a few times a week at the local gym. On occasion I would bump into a gentleman there who had an Ironman bag. We struck up a few conversations, and I asked him for advice for my first race. He said that there was one thing to know about going into an Ironman: "Somewhere between mile fifteen and twenty on the run, you are going to go into a dark place. Just know that it's coming."

If that sounds ominous, it's because it is. But it resonated with me and was some of the best advice I received for the race. It resonated because

I knew some of what to expect in my dark place. Everyone's dark place may look different, but themes run across them. In your dark place, you question your capability and you question your value: any confidence or belief in yourself cracks.

My dark place has a feeling of despondency and sadness, where I question the point and purpose of things, regret past mistakes, and feel overwhelming guilt for things that I shouldn't feel guilty about. I get filled with feelings of fear and expectations of inevitable failure. There are some people who succeed because they want to try new things; however, I succeed because I hate failure and have a fear of being left behind.

My dark place comes and goes. It's worse than melancholy but not a full-blown depression where I want to take my life. It hits me at odd times, and it's almost cyclical. My dark place finds me at some point every four to six weeks. It shows up, lasts for a day or two, and sidelines me. I can now recognize it for what it is, so I know that it will go away. Any random thing can trigger it: a sarcastic remark, an innocuous and innocent line in a speech or video I'm listening to, an unnerving interaction with a stranger. It's sometimes quite a surprise. But what gets me out of it is knowing that it will end.

The reason you hit a dark place in a long triathlon is that after swimming, biking, and running for as long as you have (up to fourteen hours), you still have another ten to twelve miles left—that can take another two hours. Your brain and body are exhausted, you're cold, and all you want is to stop and eat three or four full pizzas and go to bed. Your despondency hits, with your brain taunting you that the training you did for a year wasn't enough or the effort you put in today wasn't good enough—or both . . .

My friend Alan shared with me the old saying, "When you are painting a fence, just paint the fence." It's a reminder to be present and focus on what you can control in the moment. It's true for managing change, and it's true for finishing an Ironman. When you're swimming over two miles, you can't be worried about your bike ride. When you're biking, you can't be worried about your run. You have to be aware of them but focus on what you're doing in that moment to get to the next.

And that's what happened when I reached my dark place— fortunately for me, it wasn't until around mile twenty-two. It was difficult, but I was able to deal with it because I knew it was coming. I didn't know in advance what exactly my dark place was going to look like, I didn't know what exactly I was going to be dealing with, but I knew that it was coming at some point around the bend.

I don't know if I would have finished the race if I didn't have that awareness mindset going in. I'd been racing for twelve hours, with four miles left. I was able to comprehend what was happening. I recognized my dark place for what it was and responded appropriately.

I finished the race. It took me longer than most other racers, but in a solo event, you're only racing yourself. It's one of my biggest accomplishments, which I would never have thought possible. If you knew me twenty years before, around a cloud of cigarette smoke and buckets of booze, you wouldn't have thought it possible either.

When I remember and draw on my history, I can get out of my dark place. Yes, I trained for the Ironman and could have failed, but I had a vision in my head of showing people that I finished. I knew the faster I got to the finish line, the faster I could crawl into bed. I knew the feeling I would have of not finishing and how that would eat at me forever. It may sound silly, but for the final four miles of the race, I interviewed myself, as if I were the host of a talk show. I interviewed the Jim who finished the race, and I asked how it felt, what I learned, and whether I would do it again. It worked.

The lessons I learned about myself and from myself by doing the race are myriad. From the day I told myself it could be done to responding to a challenge in the moment, it's something I can draw on forever; it helps drive my perspective on what's possible.

"What's possible" is the theme I want to drive home. When we think about how the macro environment impacts the micro-you, we start to think about how this change affects us in our own particular ways. And this is how we manage macro change: by focusing on our micro-self.

There are problems and there are circumstances. Problems can be solved and circumstances can only be responded to: articulating the difference between the two is important. Many of us try to treat change like a problem to be solved—but there isn't a solution. It can't be "fixed." It's something to acknowledge and adapt to. Like Viktor Frankl

(2006) said in ***Man's Search for Meaning***, "You can't control circumstances, but you can control how you respond."

In order to effectively respond, however, you need to have some kind of awareness of who you are as an individual. You have to tap into your values and motivations to discover how you like to learn and what you're capable of doing. You need to articulate and define your personality—what makes that fun is that personality has multiple definitions.

At a fundamental level, personality is who we are. This includes our above-mentioned values and motivations and how we act and prioritize. It's built according to our experiences and worldviews. It's all those answers that a person gives when someone asks, "Who are you?"

But at the same time, personality is who you are according to other people. While you may think you're a confident, empathetic, and interesting individual, other people may see an arrogant chauvinist who makes them want to bang their heads against the wall. Those two definitions are quite different. But both definitions need to be laid out for you to move forward.

The different definitions happen for several different reasons. One of the big ones is that we tend to give ourselves credit for intentions and not moral actions. For example, I may think I'm thoughtful because I intended to send you a birthday card, even though I didn't. You would think the opposite, because you never heard from me and assumed that I just forgot you. Needless to say, thinking something doesn't get you credit.

The above thinking has broad implications for not only how it drives and interacts with your response mechanism but also how other people help you with your response mechanism. How you project yourself becomes a habit and is a decision that you make daily. Who you are is more than just wearing a suit and driving a BMW. It's more than your stuff; there's a mentality that needs to manifest within you.

Manifesting a mentality is a process. It's not just having an awareness of where you are today or where you want to be but understanding the steps and having a belief that you can take those steps to get from point A to B. In other words, it requires *self-efficacy*.

Self-efficacy is the brainchild of Albert Bandura; it's a psychological theory that outlines a person's assessment of "how well one can execute courses of action required to deal with prospective situations" (Bandura 1982). In essence, it's your belief that you know and can do what it takes to achieve something. It's not a confidence in yourself, per se, but rather an understanding that you have the capacity and ability to control the behaviors necessary to get to your point B. Self-efficacy isn't your self-image, your view of yourself. It transcends many aspects of the self (self-confidence, self-regulation, self-belief, self-esteem) but sits in the middle. It's a belief that you are able, that you are up to the challenge of whatever comes your way.

Self-efficacy is a game-changing psychological theory. People with high levels of self-efficacy find themselves leading organizations because they can articulate a vision, take on new challenges and succeed, and complete such things as Ironman races. Having a vision of what it takes to get something done puts you light years ahead of the competition. And to increase levels of self-efficacy, you need to focus—as usual—on yourself.

Focusing on ourselves sounds simple but is infinitely complex. There's a reason self-discovery is often compared to a journey: we take steps towards self-awareness right up to unearthing and facing the uncomfortable details we like to keep hidden. This path of self-discovery can be long and arduous. Sometimes we have to recognize some inconvenient or difficult truths, such as how our use of alcohol is impacting our ability to succeed; while other times it's discovering new loves, such as reading classic novels (that I was supposed to read in high school). We must learn to embrace the fact that we all have problems but at the same time understand that nobody, no matter who they are, has all of their shit together.

When I think of impressive individuals, individuals who I'd want to be around when the shit hits the fan, there are a lot of attributes I would use to describe them: impressive, opinionated, tactful, and other leadership-oriented words. The people I want to be around are always in control: They exude confidence because they're comfortable in their own skin. They keep their cool because they can focus on what's important. They can be flexible because their internal compass is guiding them. If they're thrown in a room with strangers, they're just fine because they know who they are inside and aren't about to compromise that for anybody.

Therefore, to respond appropriately to change and to understand our own capability to adapt, we need to focus on who we are as individuals. Becoming self-aware is fundamental to adapting. Part 2 will help you do just that.

Part Two: Be Prepared

The aim of life is self-development. To realize one's nature perfectly—that is what each of us is here for.

—Oscar Wilde, *The Picture of Dorian Gray*

Chapter 7: Prepare to Prepare

In 1957 Dwight D. Eisenhower said in a speech, "Plans are worthless, but planning is everything."

In war, your best laid plans rarely, if ever, go according to plan. Going through the exercise of planning and preparation, however, gives you the ability to respond quickly and better adapt when it goes haywire.

We respond appropriately when properly prepared because our brain isn't panicked when the time comes to make a decision. When we're calm, we think clearly; when we think clearly, we make better decisions. Proper preparation eliminates some doubt when problem solving. By thinking through scenarios, a confidence in and understanding of our capability emerges. A plan of action, that thing that we can control, comes into focus. We'll then likely end with a successful outcome, even if that result looks different than what we envisioned. If nothing else, we have less regret and can sleep better at night.

Preparation for change isn't just a plan to follow but rather an alignment, readying you to pivot at any given moment. Through proper preparation, we improve our circumstances, and therefore increase confidence and understanding of our capabilities. Ultimately, this leads us to make the right decisions.

My frustration with my place in the corporate world wasn't because of a bad organization or a shitty boss—it was because of me. Yes, I worked hard and did good work, but I wasn't easy to manage. I wasn't doing the type of work I wanted to do because I didn't try to do it; I didn't articulate what I wanted my career path to look like because I didn't know where I wanted to go. I was waiting for someone to just give me the greatest projects in the world and then recognize my all-encompassing greatness. Changing just one of these would have put my career on a different trajectory.

My frustration in the dating world wasn't entirely because I had incompatible girlfriends (though, that was often the case) but because I wasn't attracting the people I wanted to attract . . . because of me. My own insecurity didn't allow me to trust others, so I blamed others for my frustration with decisions that I made. My circle of people centered around a beer garden (which is fun, when not abused, by the way), but I wasn't spending time in a place that was littered with great productivity. To attract the people that were going to take me to another level, I had to change where I was spending my time and how I spent it because the right people weren't going to just come to me.

Ethical philosophy has a concept called *enlightened self-interest*: by serving the needs of others, you're serving the needs of yourself. It's a notion that has always held sway with me and is a lovely theory, but in reality, it isn't always possible.

To survive in the new economy, we need that type of thinking, but I believe the concept works best if you flip it on its head: by focusing on and serving the needs of the best *you*, you can help serve the needs of others. The concept works best if you take the time and do the work to first understand you.

Descriptive words, such as *leadership*, *strength*, *wisdom*, and *integrity*, all have lexical definitions but contain many connotations. We hear them all of the time in corporate slogans and inspirational quotations, but we like to use the words as descriptions of ourselves. However, what the words "look" like and what we want from them is different to everyone; therefore, we must define them for ourselves to show others (and ourselves) what we mean.

If you have to inform someone that you're wise or that you're a leader, then you're not wise or a leader. We have to show our virtues, so people believe it and *feel* it. To properly show people that we're capable of leadership or value creation in the new economy, we must show the right behaviors—that is, being intentional about our actions or lack of actions.

I know (through a lot of trial and error) that on days where I run in the morning, I treat people differently. I'm more patient and more thoughtful. I know that by going to bed at nine o'clock, I can wake up early and be much more productive in the morning, which influences the rest of the day. I know that on days I eat a box of cookies or a loaf of bread, my exhaustion rises and I don't act the way I want to. I know that if I have a beer or glass of wine, I feel it for two days.

I've learned that I have patterns; I know how to recognize those patterns by paying attention to what I'm doing, what I need, and how it influences others. Now, all my decisions are designed to make me the best possible person to the people around me—friends and strangers alike. I'm not an expert at it, and I mess up from time to time, but I have an internal guide.

Preparing for the Unknown

We can prepare for two things: what we know and what we don't. For example, we know when there's an upcoming algebra test. We wouldn't use a civics textbook to study for it; we know that there are going to be questions on the test that are algebraic in nature, so we study algebraic equations to prepare. It makes sense: we have context, we roughly know what to expect, and we move forward.

The other type of preparation for the unknown is different. Preparing for change is so large and cloudy that making specific arrangements is difficult. Instead, we should prepare for uncertainty, and that requires flexibility. We prepare so that we can be calm and make good decisions; we prepare so that we can change the circumstances on which we operate. The plan is to set ourselves up to be successful.

I'll use a sports analogy to make the point. I want you to stick with me (I know some people hate sports analogies, but this one is different and really good).

The book *Moneyball* tells the story of Billy Beane, the general manager of the Oakland Athletics (A's for short), a Major League Baseball team (Lewis 2004). Billy was hired and tasked with one thing: win. The A's weren't a successful team, so it was a tall order. They were little fish in a big pond—competing with big market, big budget teams like the Yankees and the Red Sox, without having either the big market or the big budget to attract the top, big name players.

The A's needed to think differently. They were investing in young players, developing them, and once they got really good, teams like the Yankees or Red Sox would swoop in and buy them away. That wasn't going to change—it's how the sport works. If I'm a good baseball player, I'm following the paycheck. It's the way baseball has worked since forever.

And since that circumstance wasn't going to change, Billy had to think differently about the people he was focused on acquiring. Looking at his budget and at his task (which was to win), he realized he was concentrating on the wrong area. To win you need to score runs. And rather than developing the next big star that could hit a home run every few days, he focused on bringing in the people that could consistently help him score more runs. He happened upon circumstance.

If I get a hit in baseball, that's great. I get to stand on first, second, or third base and wait for the next batter. But if I get that same hit, and *someone is already on base*, then the team's chances of scoring a run are multiples higher. One hit, two very different results.

So, Billy set out to find the people who could position the team to score more runs on little hits, which happen far more often in a baseball game. He stopped looking for people who had a lot of power, like those who hit thirty to forty home runs a year, which is what everyone else was doing.

The strategy worked. More runs were scored, more wins were had, and he took the team to the World Series. Billy is now known as the person who changed a sport by bringing analytics and a new view into the way "things were done." It's a fantastic lesson as we prepare for change. To get better solutions, we need to ask better questions.

Change is like the Red Sox baseball team: we don't like it but it will always be there. We can't do anything about that. We may not be able to compete with them on budget, but we can look at what we're doing to put our people on the bases. By increasing the chance of success when we get up to bat, we're light years ahead of others in scoring runs. And that's what we're ultimately talking about—scoring more runs.

This chapter is a challenging one, both to write and to put into practice. When we talk about things like preparation, wellness, and changing habits, we get emotional charges from the past and our judgmental mindset locks in.

We don't learn about ourselves from other people, who say things like "Be happier." We can't learn to be happy from other people. What we learn is based on what they give us to internalize, ponder, and come to a self-realization. That's one of the big secrets about change. Any change you make has to come from self-realization. You need your "Aha!" moment to make this work. My happiness and your happiness are very different things, so I would never presume to tell you to just "follow my plan."

Part 2 is what I've learned over the past two decades, packaged into a nice little guide. The guide is what I learned when I tried to understand my value and deal with my "dark place" while struggling with alcohol; it's the realizations that came to me as I resented my work, frustrated that my career in the corporate world wasn't what I wanted it to be; it's where my head got to in terms of my self-image, my role in relationships, my social standing. I wasn't well, and that needed to change.

This guide is about building the proper mindset. I want to change the way you think about things, about building self-efficacy (that psychological theory I discussed in the last chapter). I want to help you build a belief in your ability. But you must begin by thinking through the basic things that you take for granted.

We live in a time of information overload and unsolicited advice: everything from the food you eat to the friends you should have to the way you should "love yourself." All of it is bullshit. It's marketing, through someone else's filter, designed to tap into that emotion where you feel you aren't what you want to be.

But you can be. And that's what I figured out. There are ways that you can rethink things your way. None of this is extreme. But by figuring out you, you'll be able to tackle any change that comes your way—you'll be prepared.

The following four sections focus on readying you for the new economy: physical, mental, social, and financial preparation. They cover everything you need to adapt to a new economy. Each of these components will have an impact on the others. Your physical preparation impacts your mental and social preparation. Your financial preparation has major implications on your social and mental preparation.

I'm giving you the why in this book, and what it meant to me. I can't give you the what and the how. It's the mistake many people make. For me to tell you what you should eat or how to think about yourself is disingenuous. It's where most change programs fail: I'm a square peg, you're a round hole.

But I'll give you plenty to think about. Your role is to figure out how these four ways to prepare relate to you and the changes you can make—you *will* make changes, O Self-Efficacious One. We're making a psychological shift to what's important, one that's not consumer in nature and can't be bought in a store. It's your mindset, it's your shell, and it's how you can present your best self to the people around you. The lessons learned, and the work you do after reading these chapters in part 2, will help you figure out your path, no matter the change any economy sends your way.

Like Eisenhower said, planning is everything. Because of this, life almost feels like a boot camp—and in a way it is.

CHAPTER 8: PHYSICAL PREPARATION

Relax—there's no running (unless you want there to be).

Why is physical preparation so challenging? Just the idea of physical preparation comes saddled with assumptions. When we hear or see the words *diet*, *fitness*, and *sleep*, we think of unsolicited advice from other people; as a result, our listening and curiosity turns off.

We think about why we "can't" do something rather than whether we should. We find the one thing wrong with a good idea to show why it will never work for us: "I have a bad knee, so I can't go running; therefore, I will not work out ever." The logic isn't quite there, but we believe it regardless.

Physical preparation isn't about making you into Adonis, guzzling protein shakes, going vegan, and working out seven days a week. But if that's what you want, by all means, go ahead. Physical preparation is about fine-tuning your system, tapping into what's going to make you operate at your top level. Your system runs on three things: the fuel that makes you go, the vessel that you're in, and the sleep you need to repair.

Yes, what you look like impacts not only how people view you but also how you view yourself. We know that good-looking and fit people get treated better than not-good-looking people; we know that overweight people face prejudices that thin people don't. I'm being blunt because all of that is everyday circumstance—you're not going to change it, you're not going to fix it, and you can't avoid it.

But it's also not a reason to ignore physical preparation. When we think of the physical, we go to how we look. It's the easiest thing to focus on. But it also has to do with how we feel. Physical preparation is so important because the way you treat yourself physically impacts your mental and social state.

I imagine you occasionally have some of the same feelings that I do. There are days where I know I'm not operating as I should be at work, and it's frustrating. Or I'll look back over the past few days and know I wasn't as productive as I should have been. I get disappointed and angry. I might question my ability. My answers to my wife and daughter can get short.

My answer to this feeling, when I recognize it, is typically in the physical realm. One of the three parts of physical preparation (diet, exercise, or sleep) is usually out of whack. Maybe I ate more carbs than usual, which zapped my focus. Maybe I was so busy I put fitness on the back burner and didn't go for the runs that I love. Maybe I didn't sleep well. Maybe it's Maybelline.

I run through my checklist. I can almost always figure out what I did that put me in that mindset. "On Tuesday we had that big pasta dinner and I didn't sleep well. That's why my Wednesday was off." Finding answers like this truly help me—I can find the cause, put it behind me, and move forward. I know it's not "me" and my ability that's causing it, but it's a decision I made that can be remedied in the future.

So, with that, I would like you to open your mind and think about your physical preparation. Yes, you can change your habits and the things you do. Yes, the best time to do this was probably twenty years ago. Yes, the second-best time to do it is now.

As I explain the three-part physical system below, I want you to think about your own questions that need answering. I'm not going to advocate a particular diet or a fitness regimen or the greatest mattress in the world. That's up to you. You're the person who can define it for you. But I'll advocate a way to think about it.

Diet

We'll start at the beginning, which is as good a place as any. What you consume has the biggest influence on all other areas. What you eat and drink drives your ability to think, desire to move, and capability to learn. It affects your sleep and the way you think about yourself. It drives how you approach your challenges and affects the glow of your skin. It impacts your interactions with people and the way other people see you. In a nutshell: physical preparation, and adapting to the new economy, starts with diet.

I'm not a nutritionist, which is why I'm not going to tell you what specifically to eat. However, I've learned, through trial and error, a common theme when making decisions about diet: do what is needed for me. I know and have experienced how my diet has affected my ability to think—for instance, I'm a person who has struggled with weight gain, so I've lived and learned through many different strategies to help me at a particular time. As the result of my troubleshooting, I've come up with three guiding principles that have helped me over time:

1) Understand what diet means.
2) Understand what food is.
3) Define moderation.

Do I stick with them always? No. Sometimes I'll eat a whole box of cookies in one sitting. Nobody is perfect. Sometimes I feel like I *need* a whole box of cookies in a short amount of time. But by focusing on those three principles (most of the time), and cutting out all of the other noise (this diet and that diet and calorie counting), my body shape has shifted back to what it was supposed to be; consequently, I'm able to think more clearly and I sleep like a baby.

Research shows that our stomach has an outsized effect on everything we do, not just processing food. What we consume, from cigarette smoke to lima beans, can influence the bacteria that drive things like serotonin, stress response, and our immune system. We're learning that there's a direct correlation between the stomach and cognitive ability, between gut bacteria and general health.

When we think of diet, we typically attribute it to weight loss. But it's so much more—it's the fuel for your thinking, for your physical activity, for your mood. Yes, there's a specialty area of psychiatry focused on diet and how it impacts your mood. I'm a perfect example: my mood swings can be legendary and last for days if my diet is off.

When I don't eat properly, my entire countenance changes. After the box of cookies, I'm less engaging, I get tired, and I'm shorter with my words. I've gotten to the point where I say to my wife, "I ate this" and she knows that I'm going to be "that Jim" for the rest of the day.

Books have been written on the psychiatric and neurological benefits of food. I won't bore you with that here. But I'll take you through my three principles and pull out what's relevant to you.

We need to be a little basic here. People are emotional when it comes to food. I encourage you to think with an open mind. Just because you're clinging to your three daily sodas, it doesn't mean that it's healthy. And that's okay. That's your choice. But so much information flies around on food, and opinion is often shared as fact. We need to define what exactly we're talking about, with no assumptions filling the gaps, on what I mean by diet.

The word *diet* is a noun. It's what you consume on a regular basis. Things are or aren't a part of your diet. Never say, "I'm going on a diet," because that implies that it ends. Your diet is sustenance; the fuel that makes your engine go.

To be extra clear, a diet isn't just what you eat. When I say "diet," it's everything that you consume and ingest into your body. It's an avocado; it's a cigarette. It's rice; it's whiskey. If it goes into your body, it will affect your body. Cigarettes and alcohol used to be a part of my diet, but not anymore.

To be blunt, many of us are consuming a lot of really shitty things. I'm guilty of it—you're likely guilty of it. And by recognizing that you're a reflection of what you consume, you need to take a look at what it is that's fueling your thinking and activity.

Everything about food is a marketer's dream. We've absolutely convoluted the discussion. We're so focused on whether we should or shouldn't eat a particular thing that we lose the big picture. Things are created and packaged and sold in a way designed to get you to eat more of whatever they create. Billions of dollars are spent researching the grocery-shopping experience in order to have you spend more time in it; even more is spent on packaging, branding, and advertising and on food scientists to create a product that you'll buy.

All of it is noise—and that's why thinking about diet and food is confusing and exhausting. It's so exhausting, with macronutrients and micronutrients and this tri and that glyceride that we just throw our hands up and look for a solution. We want someone to tell us what to do: to package it for us, to deliver it, and to think for us. With so many of us concerned about weight and hating the extra pounds we have, we're attracted to these "simple solutions" of organic this and fat-free that. But it doesn't have to be challenging. I was better off when I began to break down diet into simple concepts.

Mark Hyman is a nutritionist and doctor who has tried to set the record straight. In his very blunt book *Food: WTF Should I Eat?*, Dr. Hyman (2018) outlines a matter-of-fact, basic rule that drives his eating. According to him, our food choices come out of two buckets: "food" and "food-like substances."

Food is food: avocado, bacon, tomato, beans. A food-like substance is something different. it's the stuff created and processed and a bit too delicious to be good for you: Twinkies, soda, and nachos; these are food-like substances, not food.

It's almost too simple, but that's its beauty. We're eating buckets of garbage; things that aren't food but are marketed as such. And it's not all our fault: we're susceptible to marketing and tasty things. Entenmann's crumb cake is one of the worst things I eat, but it's one of my favorite things (and I can eat the whole thing in one sitting).

Here's another way to put it: everything you ingest is either helping you or harming you, either making you healthy or making you sick—there's no in-between. It's either beneficial or it's not. And now that we understand what food is, we can then move on to the next part: How much do I eat?

We have all heard the guidelines out there on how many calories an adult needs. But guidelines aren't rules; they must be adjusted to you. A person training for an Ironman is going to have very different calorie needs than a person who sits in front of a computer all day.

Understanding how much of what you need is the name of the game. I know people who only eat one meal a day, and that's perfect for them. Others eat throughout the day in small increments. Also fine. But experimenting with your consumption is vital to understanding what you actually need.

By not focusing on quantity, we fall into the portion-size trap. I used to pour a whole bowl of cereal for breakfast. It turns out it was four servings. So, while I thought I was only eating two hundred calories, I was eating eight hundred calories for breakfast.

Our portion sizes are massive, and we don't understand them. It's why people calorie count. It's not so you can save ten calories here or there; it's so that you understand what a portion size is.

Nickel and diming your calorie count is frustrating and fairly useless. After all, we're only estimating anyway. But when you can estimate portion size, such as a one hundred calorie portion of chicken, the way you eat will drastically change. It can be embarrassing to admit that we need to relearn how to appropriately consume food.

We always hear that "everything is okay in moderation." That's great—but what's moderation? every day? twice a day? once a week? If soda, pizza, and cheeseburgers are all "OK" in moderation, can you have one of each a day? After all, you're only having one soda that day "in moderation" and only one pizza "in moderation" and only one cheeseburger "in moderation."

It all comes down to what you're willing to sacrifice to get what you want. If you want to lose weight, is that desire bigger than the desire to eat unhealthy food? That's the only way it's going to work. For example, if you're not producing as much at the office and have a cloudy feeling when you think, think about what you're eating. There's a reason you're exhausted after lunch: you ate too much. It's time to have a real conversation with yourself about what you're consuming.

I'm not advocating an overnight revamp of what you eat. That's not realistic. My point is that we need to create guidelines and be intentional with what we consume. Turning away from all sugar and meat and eating only vegetables and nuts may help you lose weight, but it's not what your body needs. Yes, allow yourself snacks. Yes, you can eat meat. Yes, you can eat cookies and pizza. But recognize what works for you and do it in an appropriate manner. As you get more and more intentional with your diet, you'll feel different.

It's not easy. As I was writing this chapter, there were brownies in the fridge. I picked one up, but I thought, "Will this brownie help me or harm me?" And then I ate the brownie. It happens. But we can still do what we can to make the best possible choices. Our dietary choices help us make better choices elsewhere in our lives. And diet leads us to the next topic: fitness.

(One last note before we go to the next section: eat your damn vegetables.)

Fitness

I promised there wouldn't be running, and I meant it. Just like diet, fitness has gone completely overboard, with gym memberships going unused; new, fashionable ways to work out popping up everywhere; and $125 Lululemon yoga pants to go to the supermarket (my wife added that last one).

Like diet, I'm going to keep this one simple: (1) you need to find something active that you can do every day, (2) you have to learn how to do it properly, and (3) you have to learn how to love it.

That's it.

It could be walking or running or weightlifting; it could be pushups, sit-ups, cycling, swimming, tennis. It doesn't matter. The only question you should be asking yourself each day regarding fitness is, Was I active today?

We need to move our muscles. We need to burn calories. We need to elevate our heart rate to improve blood flow and to increase oxygen throughout the body. You don't have to run a marathon, *but you need to do something*.

The neurological benefits are there. Research shows that an increase in physical activity is related to a decrease in stress and anxiety, improved cognitive development, better academic performance, improved memory, and additional ability in processing emotions. As we think about being flexible in a new economy, we need to prioritize fitness.

I've learned to love running. What got me over the hump was knowing how great I would feel when it was over. I feel accomplished and well. And now I'm well beyond that; I do my best thinking while running. I go for a run when I need to work through a problem. I enjoy it in the moment, and the act of running is now something that I enjoy. But to get there took me a long time.

I always wanted to create a physical routine. I was an active kid, but I stopped at high school, and after picking up drinking and smoking habits in college, I never went back. However, when I saw people who were fit and healthy, I wanted to be like them. So, I did what most people would do—I started to run on a treadmill. I did it for fifteen minutes, got wiped out, felt accomplished, and moved on. It didn't do anything for me.

Then I would try to run outside. I wouldn't be able to make it a mile. I would get frustrated, go back inside, drink a beer, and say, "At least I tried." I would then go back to my nonphysical routine because any kind of physical activity was awful. But it was awful because I didn't know what I was doing or why I was doing it.

I can pinpoint the times where my fitness psychology changed. I had a moment where I recognized that I could do it, a moment where I learned how to do it, and a moment I fell in love with it.

A challenge I have in believing that I can do just about anything is that I sign up for stupid things. If you float a stupid idea by me, like skydiving, there's a good chance I'm going to do it. And a few years ago, at the beginning of the mud-running craze, I found something stupid to sign up for: Tough Mudder.

At the time, a Tough Mudder race was a twelve-mile run through mud with thirty obstacles, such as climbing walls and electric shocks. In retrospect, it was stupid, but it was a lot of fun. And it was particularly beneficial for me because it forced me to accomplish something.

After convincing a few friends to do it with me, I went forward. I didn't sleep the night before because I didn't know what to expect. I also knew that running twelve miles wasn't going to happen (I couldn't run one). I figured that I could walk if I had to and that all I had to do was show up and do my best.

I did it. I was miserable, but I did it. It was cold, it was in smelly New Jersey water, and it was dirty. But I made it to the end and have the headband to prove it. And as I reflected on the day, I was shocked that I didn't even notice that I had run twelve miles (because we were going so slow and had breaks at the obstacles) and that I didn't even hesitate. I technically had a twelve-mile run in the books: I knew I could do more.

I started running every once in a while. I would go slow—I told myself to keep a Tough Mudder pace. And I was able to run longer distances. I still wasn't great, but I was able to get it done. But then, by way of a random run in France, I had my second moment: I learned how to run.

When I'm on vacation, for some reason, I have the sudden urge to be healthy. It's this weird backwards thing for me: I eat like garbage throughout the year and then go on vacation and try to eat salad. In that vein, when on vacation, I usually try to go for a run in the morning.

I went for a run in Lyon, France, at about six in the morning. I was going down the street when I saw a lady running about a block ahead of me. I didn't know why I noticed her, until I realized that she was running with what looked like no effort. I tried to figure out what she was doing, and it hit me—she was running on her toes, which is what my grandfather always told me to do when I was a young boy.

She turned down a road and I kept going. I got to the end of a street and as I turned around to go back to my hotel, I decided to run on my toes. I felt so incredibly awkward, but I also knew that it was the right way to run—it just felt right. I practically flew the rest of the way to my hotel. It changed the way I run forever.

I had been trying to force a running habit, and the reason it wasn't working was because I didn't know how to run. It sounds ridiculous that I might need to learn something so basic as how to run, but learning to do an exercise properly is fundamental to be successful with it. So now knowing I could run and changing the way I did it put me on a path to embrace running.

Over time, I learned to absolutely love it. My weekend mornings generally revolve around a five-to-ten-mile run. It's where I do my best thinking; it's what calms me down. I've been able to witness a change in mood and productivity according to whether I'm physically active in the morning.

You must take the following three steps for whatever you want to do: (1) pick an activity, (2) recognize that you can do it (even though you may not be doing it well at the beginning), and (3) focus on learning how to do it (ask questions and be open to feedback). And as you improve and challenge yourself in different ways, fitness will become a part of your identity.

I'm a completely different person on days where I get my physical activity in—whether it's running, boxing, cycling, swimming, or weights. I've gotten to the point where I know I have to do something for the benefit of my mentality and psychology, and I change it up from day-to-day. Now I do it when I'm struggling with something. I'm a completely different person.

Sleep

The final aspect of physical preparation is sleep.

It's one of those things that's easiest to sacrifice. We work hard all day, so to unwind, we relax with television or a book at night. We're stressed about work, so we toss and turn. Making sleep a priority seems incongruous with getting things done, yet the research shows that sleep is one of the top drivers of productivity.

Our sleep is our reset button. It heals us physically and mentally. It's when the body and brain can go to work and help us through whatever we're dealing with.

I like to use a file cabinet as an example. When we wake up, we start to pull files from the filing cabinet. You walk to the bathroom and pick up a toothbrush: your brain has pulled out the "Toothbrush" file. You walk down the street and recognize an old friend: it pulls the "College Friend" file. You go to the office and start plugging away: it pulls the "Pain-in-the-Ass Client" file.

Our brain pulls all these files throughout the day to help with our processes or memory. Some files are easy to find because we use them all the time, like our toothbrush file or our "I Need to Wear Pants" file. Others are wayyyyyyy in the back, like that person you saw on the street from twenty years ago and you can't remember their name.

But just because your brain pulls these files out, it doesn't mean that it puts them back; your brain is too busy. Once you're done brushing your teeth, it's already pulling out the shower file. At the end of the day, your mind looks like Einstein's office, with files scattered all over the place. It's in our sleep where the cleaning crew comes in and puts everything back to where it should be. Without organizing your files, you find yourself staring at a problem that should be easy, but it isn't. You can't find that file.

We have a natural sleep cycle. It's driven by sunlight, activity, electrical impulses of the planet, and all kinds of other things. We've had this cycle for thousands of years, which we'll continue to have. No, most of us aren't farmers, but we've a natural response to the world around us that we tend to disrupt.

Just like diet and fitness, we can only do our best. There are going to be nights where you can't go to bed early or you can't sleep late. That's life. But prioritizing sleep, recognizing its value, will help you make better decisions throughout your day and respond in better ways to what is coming at you.

For me, the two best things that drive my sleep are (get ready) . . . my diet and my exercise. When all three are in sync—diet, exercise, and sleep—good things happen, especially with how I think and what I need mentally to prepare for life.

Chapter 9: Mental Preparation

When thinking of responding to the new economy—and to change in general—we're really talking about a new way to think: a shift in our psychology that allows us to analyze, comprehend, and make good decisions. We saw in the last chapter how your physical preparation can impact your thoughts.

We need to build up our psychological capital in order to benefit ourselves in the workplace, marketplace, community, and home. We need to increase our capacity to recognize that our value is strong, our capability is sound, and our direction in life is centered.

Mental health is a gargantuan topic and a very serious one. I'm not going to address mental illness in this book, because I'm not the right person or properly equipped to do so. There are professionals who specialize in those areas, and my opinions on that would be mostly untrained; however, I've dealt with mental health issues on my own, and I've found that many people have shared the same experiences.

Mental health goes far beyond what we typically see. Everyone on this planet has been impacted, either directly or indirectly, by mental health issues. Some issues are more serious than others: depression, alcoholism, drug use, a paralyzing fear of failure, and so much more. Outside of many conditions, much mental health is scalable—on some days, or for different people, it's worse than others.

My mental health is a roller-coaster ride. Before my epiphany, I struggled with a view of myself, so I used destructive methods to deal with it. Some days would be great and I would have a high, while other days I would be very low. I called those days my "dark place." I would have feelings of abject sadness and fear of the unknown. I felt like an imposter and a failure. There were days and evenings where I would sit, drink, and smoke in my home, either resenting that I didn't live up to what I could or distracting myself from taking the difficult actions to become what I could.

I couldn't create a vision of where I wanted to go because I didn't really know where I was.

The question isn't about what mental health *is*, it's about how we deal with it that makes the difference. It's creating an inner dialogue to find out who we are, what we need, and where we want to go. It's shifting the conversation from a bigger view (e.g., What's going on around me?) to a specific view (e.g., What do I need to do right now to move forward?). Everyone has made mistakes, everyone has fucked up royally at least once, and nobody can change that. It's in the past; it's learning; we move on.

When I hit my wall and had my epiphany, and continued to reflect on me—who I was and what I wanted—a bright light shone onto what I kept in the dark. It showed me that I was wasting time allowing other people to dictate my thinking and actions, and when I allowed other people so much power to impact my decisions, my thinking was inhibited. On reflection, I found that there were three areas where I needed to focus; interestingly, they all revolved around me.

A big hang-up for many people (and I was especially one of those people) is constant concern over "what other people will think." You'd be surprised about how your imaginary thought of what another imaginary person might think will impact your decisions. My epiphany really helped me realize that other opinions are generally meaningless and irrelevant—I needed to focus on what I thought about myself, what I needed in a given moment, and what I truly believed.

Mental health wellness and preparation are just like physical health: they require ongoing attention. Mental and physical aren't the same, yet they are inextricably linked. What keeps someone "well" differs from person to person. The statement "you need to focus on self-care" doesn't mean anything; defining self-care for you, and starting on the learning journey of what you need is the name of the game. I went through the process, and I'm continuing to go through it every day.

There are three aspects to mental wellness: self-love, self-care, and your belief system.

My initial reaction to hearing the terms *self-love* and *self-care* was that they're some of the softest, flightiest, biggest pieces of bullshit commentary that exist. I come from a place where you put your head down, do your work, quit your bitching, and move on. You don't talk about feelings and you don't talk about emotions—you deal with your shit and focus forward.

But in my journey of discovery, I realized that those terms accurately described what I was learning. Especially when things get challenging, we begin to question who we are and what we're capable of doing. It's uncomfortable. Realizations that feelings and emotions are to be dealt with productively, not ignored, were a bit of a game changer for me. But I needed to define those soft words into something I could respond to. This is where I landed:

1. Self-love is when you embrace your imperfections and recognize that you have value.
2. Self-care is when you're aware of and recognize what you need, in the moment.
3. Your belief system consists of the core of who you are as an individual.

Let's unwrap these lovely gifts; they have nuance.

Self-Love

Self-love is the softest sounding of the three. I used to think it was for hippies and weak children. If you asked me ten, fifteen, twenty years ago, my opinion about self-love would have been that people needed to just get over themselves, move on, and get shit done. However, once I allowed myself to grow and learn it for myself, I realized how far off the mark I was.

In essence, I believe that self-love means having respect for yourself. Or, as Jean-Jacques Rousseau ([1782] 1953) writes in his book *The Confessions* my favorite quote of all time: "How can anyone be satisfied in life if they aren't satisfied with the one person they can't be separated from?"

Think back to a person that you loved or still love more than anything—your child, your partner, or a friend. You would do anything for them. You would drop anything and be at their side in a moment if they needed it. Are you willing to give yourself that attention as well?

Self-love is a challenge and difficult because you know all your secrets. You know your self-doubts; you don't see them in other people. You don't normally see the mistakes that the people in front of you made ten years ago, yet you remember yours and they gnaw at your confidence. You don't see other people's indecision—yet you feel your own.

Are you able to take things from the past, recognize them as lessons or forgive yourself, and move on? Are you able to take your self-doubt and recognize that only *you* see it, nobody else? Are you comfortable in your own skin, to be who you want to be? We all want to be this way, yet we struggle. Answering these questions is a good exercise to go through.

Figuring out the self-love thing was groundbreaking for me. If I hadn't figured this out, there's no way I would have gotten married, started a business, or completed an Ironman.

My life before the epiphany was a story of guilt and insecurity. I almost constantly dealt with imposter syndrome: everyone else seemed smarter, faster, better looking, funnier; I never felt like I belonged. My self-image was cracked; I was overweight and felt unhealthy. If a mistake happened, I felt overwhelming guilt, even if it wasn't my fault. I was constantly operating "in the service of others" to my own detriment. I wasn't serving others, I was a servant to others. I was letting them dictate my life.

At the same time, I had an inflated sense of what should come to me. Since I was working so much for other people, and not myself, I built up resentment when promotions or raises didn't come my way. And since I didn't know how to articulate my value, I stewed. It became a cycle of not articulating what I wanted, then not getting it, then resenting it, which led to negative interactions, which led to more not articulating what I wanted.

I initially got quiet; I operated under the principle that the less you say, the smarter people think you are. But with frustration and insecurity taking over, I took an easier route and became viciously sarcastic. I put people and their ideas down because I wanted to appear "superior" to them. I never looked for an opportunity to do more than what I had to.

I didn't have an issue with doing work. My issue was that I was waiting for people to give me the recognition I thought I deserved. But when you wait for someone else to articulate your value for you, you're going to be disappointed. Think about it—we're so busy dealing with our own chaos, who has time to worry about someone else's problems?

It sounds harsh, but nobody cares as much as you do.

Without that external validation, that recognition, I drank . . . heavily. When you drink, you're the smartest person in the room. You have the answers to all of the problems, and everything makes sense. And when you surround yourself with other drinkers, you fill that void.

If I was home alone, I would drink in a state of elevated depression, an echo chamber of a cloudy mind, frustrated with where I was in life. Some nights I cried. There were nights where I wanted to be sad; it was as if I had created this ongoing desire for self-pity. If I went out, I was a very popular person at the bar, buying drinks and faking through that validation. Strangers will tell you whatever you want to hear if you're picking up the tab.

I didn't realize how much it was affecting me until I stopped. In a moment of clarity, I realized that all the great ideas I had when drinking went nowhere. No matter what thoughts I had or problems I "solved" at night, nothing changed in the morning. It was an ongoing circle of false productivity and change.

Your problem may not be drinking. It could be sex; it could be social media. Many of us try to use something that will fill that void of external validation. But at the end of the day, after you reflect on it, nothing changes and that void is still there—because the void is within ourselves.

Recognizing your value, your motivations, and your capabilities is not only cathartic but also freeing. You start to give yourself the validation that you're craving. And once you start to validate yourself, and give yourself that license to be yourself, you start to attract those people that will be additive and beneficial to your life. After all, how can you expect someone else to love you if you don't love yourself?

It's easier said than done. Much of this void and the habits protecting it are decades in the making. We have to be creative in how we're changing our mindset; it will potentially upend how we live. Relationships will end, but new ones will start. Changing your thinking is an effective way to move forward.

I like to think that I flipped a switch and all was good. But that's not the case. I still have those feelings of inferiority and insecurity; however, I've created tools to help me deal. My favorite is my positivity document.

I have (at the moment) a seven-page document on my phone that I carry everywhere with me. On it, I've written out the person who I want to be, and also I continually add in statements or moments where I felt like I was living that person. It's compliments from old bosses, and it's statements from friends. It's a list of some of the things I've done that I'm most proud of. It also has some things that I'm not: I put in the lessons I've learned to help keep me on the right path.

Reviewing our accomplishments, compliments, and successes makes it easier to embrace our imperfections. It's easier to then forgive yourself for mistakes you make (and those you don't). It's a confidence booster when you need it and a reminder of your capability and power. I review mine often before big client meetings, before networking events, on random Saturday mornings, and so on.

The journey for self-love is ongoing for me. Positivity documents help, but most of my change happened over time, with an open and curious mind on what I needed in the moment. I had brief stints of therapy and coaching, which helped me think differently on what I was doing. The person I am today is light-years away from the person I was a decade ago.

There's power in self-love. It's about knowing at the end of each day that you're going to be okay. That no matter the struggle, no matter the challenge you're faced with, you're comfortable with the choices you've made.

Self-love is about recognizing that you have value—to others and to yourself. It's not self-adulation: this isn't about false confidence or arrogance. It's about having respect, love, and trust, which will lead into care.

Self-Care

As self-love is tapping into and embracing your attributes, self-care is about meeting the mental needs you have over time. When I say self-care, I mean mental relief. We need a break from stress, mayhem, and everything else. Not only is the break from stress important but also it's vital to know when you need it.

I'll start with what annoys me about self-care: everyone seems to be an expert on what you need or when you need it. Once you focus on self-care and have an awareness of what you need and when you need it, you'll suddenly be very aware when other people start dictating what you need. Unless they've dealt with everything you're dealing with, and have had the same experiences as you, they can take their advice and shove it up their self-cared-for ass.

You dictate your own care. You're the person who knows what stress relief is for you. You're the person who knows when things get overwhelming for you. You're the person who has specific triggers that drive stress and exhaustion. For some people, a break is needed daily, others weekly, others at complete random.

Here's why we need a break: the negative health impacts of stress are well known, but in the context of the changing economy, stress pushes us towards negative personality attributes that aren't helpful. Dr. Robert Hogan, founder of the Hogan Personality Assessments, calls these negative attributes the "dark side" of personality: those negative behaviors to watch for when stress levels increase. These behaviors are called "derailers," because they upend relationships, ruin reputations, and disrupt a success track (Hogan Assessments, n.d.).

Outside of learning new habits, the way we avoid the dark side is through self-care; it's about taking steps to tap into the parasympathetic nervous system, otherwise known as the stress-reducing nervous system. We operate in two modes, and two modes only: stress and relief. Some stress is good—it motivates us to act; relief and care allow us to catch our breath.

There are many ways to do it. Research has shown that finding ongoing activities to stimulate our minds and keep us refreshed are directly linked to our mental wellness. It's not just focusing on self-care "when we need it," it's an ongoing balance over time. Put some energy in the bank and pull from it when you need it. Physical activities are typical examples (like long distance running), but hobbies and interests as well. You get to dictate what you do on your break: reading, going for a walk, or a cup of tea with a friend are all options. For some, a pet helps; for others, it's a walk in the woods. To help you find your self-care tactics, think about the things that you do where you lose track of time. As we will see in part 3 "Be Teachable," one of the benefits of learning new things is that learning new things helps relieve stress; also, it helps us change our views.

I wrote about some of the challenges facing change, in particular the needs of a mindset shift that needs to happen. Part of our self-care has to do with this mindset shift. Yes, we can jump on the seesaw and go from stress to relief, but the uncomfortable jump becomes easier to take when the swing isn't so extreme.

As the aforementioned "unwritten contract" in part 1 is being rewritten—that change we experience affects our expectations and visions of success—we need to shift our focus to what we're learning and are capable of doing, not what's being hypothetically taken away. The people who hold themselves accountable for their well-being will have the lesser swings. In a weird juxtaposition, those who take the most responsibility for themselves have greater satisfaction, which leads to a healthier stress balance.

The modern economy was built on consumption, but it's not sustainable going forward. Everything is built to be used and disposed of as quickly as possible. And it's not just products—it's our entrepreneurial mindset as well. I see that more and more people aren't starting "businesses," they're starting "their new project." The language we're using in our adventures and initiatives are implicitly short-term as well.

Personal prioritization has to shift from a short-term productivity mindset to a satisfaction mindset. It's the happiness equation: happiness equals expectation plus satisfaction. We know what happiness is and how to get it. Typically, when we say we aren't happy, it's because we aren't satisfied with where we are in life. And when you call happiness "satisfaction," or a question of your expectation, it becomes an easier challenge to address. "Why am I not satisfied?" is a simpler question to answer than "Why am I not happy?"

My grandmother had a saying: "We don't do stress." It came out mostly around Christmastime when we were planning her annual family party. With seven children and over forty grandchildren, Nanny Lyons had plenty of organizing to do, especially as she made a stocking, with gifts, for each individual at the party.

In the days leading up to the party, we would hear the mantra "we don't do stress" repeated often. It was her way of remembering what was important—seeing family—against whatever challenge came with such a large gathering. It's something that will always stick with her grandchildren, and I find myself saying it out loud often.

It's a good mantra for you as you define your self-care: I don't do stress. Finding that true break—a break for you for however long you need it—will provide wonders as you navigate change. And that's important, because we're about to talk about your belief system, which may end up changing who you are as an individual.

Belief System

Your belief system is next level shit—and my favorite part of this entire book.

It's super fun for me because it's the thinking aspect of your preparation. It's the deep type of thought that can completely upend everything you've been told or you believe. Rethinking my belief system has had one of the biggest impacts on how I respond to change: it's the creation of a filter that gives you understanding and control. Figuring out your belief system is difficult, a lot of work, and not easy in any way, shape, or form—which is why it's awesome.

Many coaches and gurus ask the question, "Who do you want to be?" We answer it, maybe with something like "Batman," and we move on. By spending the time to go deeper into your belief system, peeling back the onion seven or eight layers to get to the real crux of who you are as an individual, you benefit by forcing yourself to answer multiple questions, such as "Why?"

There's a root-cause-analysis process that businesses use called the Five Whys. When something goes wrong, or a problem exists, we ask, "Why did that happen?" Based on that answer, we then ask it again, and again, and again. After asking "Why?" five times, like a two-year-old, you will get to the root cause of whatever challenge you're facing. It's the same with what you believe. Something may not be wrong, but we need to go down a few levels of "Why?" to get to the core assumptions we're making.

Our brains like to take shortcuts. Once we create habits, or repeat thoughts over and over again, our brain doesn't stop. It's like a record, where your head says, "Yep, no need to stop here; we know what this is, let's move on." But sometimes that record needs a little scratch. And having your record spin around doesn't mean that you have a belief system in place—it just means that you're able to spit back or repeat what you've been told or heard your entire life.

Your belief system casts an extremely wide net. It could range from something as simple as what you believe when it comes to disciplining your children to as complex as how you wish to prioritize your life. It could be as superfluous as your opinion about the greatest basketball player of all time (Lebron or Jordan?) or as heavy and core focused as whether you believe God exists.

Your belief system is part of your development from adolescence to adulthood. In raising children, we try to instill values and a sense of being. At a certain point, those children need to take what they have learned and begin making decisions for themselves. Those decisions are made much easier when we understand our belief system. That doesn't mean we "know what is supposed to be done"; it means we respond in the proper way to our core. We can then defend and explain any decision we make without stress or guilt.

Part of our experiences, background, and history are things we've heard our entire lives. Being raised Irish Catholic, I had certain beliefs ingrained in me during childhood. I mean, we were *really* Irish Catholic. The only times my mother turned off a Wolfe Tones song in the car was to say the rosary as a family (on any car ride more than fifteen minutes). No meat on Fridays. Altar boy. Church every Sunday (plus, possibly, a few times during the week). You get the picture.

And being raised that way, I was surrounded by other Irish Catholics, either by spending time with my sixty first cousins or friends and neighbors from the community. People with similar belief systems congregate together.

But as we get older, many people never question those beliefs. After all, they were just told to us as we were growing up. You went to church because you had to; you became an altar boy because everyone else did. You carry those unchallenged beliefs as you grow older, have children, and pass them on.

136

But do you actively *believe* your unchallenged beliefs? Or are they just a part of your belief system? Perhaps you do—and that's great. You're part of a community with other people who believe the same things. Perhaps you don't—that's also great. It gives you something to explore and ask what you actually do believe. You also have a community of other people who may question the same beliefs.

Just because you've been told something for your entire life doesn't mean you have to believe it. No matter the topic you wish to explore (religion, politics, sports, etc.), your initial answer on what you believe isn't necessarily important. What is important is that next step: getting to the why.

The why is important because everything has a gray area, which is where your belief system comes in. And when you've thought through your belief system, and you've peeled back that onion, you can discuss your beliefs with less emotion. You can have a discussion with someone who disagrees with you and you can be open to that perspective. This is possible because, to be secure in your belief system, *you have to understand the other side.*

You can't say you believe something if you don't understand the belief opposite to your belief. I don't think you can believe in God if you don't understand how people don't. By saying you're a Democrat or Republican without understanding their perspective is something called *identity politics*—you don't listen to the other side or have educated opinions: you go with whatever the group supports. If you can't say that Republicans and Democrats can both be right a lot of the time, then you haven't done your work.

My decision-making ability has skyrocketed significantly since I've learned to challenge and question my belief system by understanding all sides. I've separated my belief system from my self-worth—they're not the same thing. What I believe is just that: a belief; it doesn't mean that someone who believes something different is wrong. I've more control over my thoughts and emotions because I understand that everyone has a belief system that will never align with me perfectly. That's fantastic.

Articulating your belief system gives you both accountability and license for your decisions. By dictating what you believe, it pulls you out of the influence of others. It allows you to do things that you perhaps would have avoided if you had listened to other people. Forging your path, making decisions for yourself, and holding yourself accountable is vital to survive the new economy.

There's one caveat: I'm going to talk more in part 3 about the prospect that you could be wrong. You must be open to the idea that you're going to make the wrong decisions sometimes, and you have to recognize that your belief system is a living thing— it will change over time. What you believe today could very well change tomorrow. That's healthy; it shows an open mind, an appreciation for new ideas and new ways to respond. Changing beliefs allows you to see a bigger picture, not just the one dictated to you or by you.

When people ask me what was the biggest challenge of becoming an entrepreneur after working in corporate for fifteen years, I tell them that I had to unlearn everything about how things were done. Many things I did were wrong. For my work, now, there are no rules. And that's wild.

It's a lot to take in. It's a lot of work—thinking and reflecting and questioning. But recognize this: once you start on this journey, your belief system will change, be based on new experiences, lead you to new people, and change things you do. These changes can rattle you to your core. It's very uncomfortable, but it's been said that if you aren't uncomfortable, you aren't improving. It's a humbling experience, which is something we all can use.

And when it comes to being served a bit of humble pie, that humbling experience is a lot easier to take when you love and care for yourself.

CHAPTER 10: SOCIAL PREPARATION

When we hear the words "physical" and "mental," we next expect to hear "spiritual." But that's not the case in preparing for the new economy. I categorize spiritual under the belief system of mental. *Spirituality* is a mental and belief exercise. Many people benefit from their spiritual exploration—so I encourage you to do so if it's right for you. But the next pillar of finding your place in the economy isn't looking up to the spirits of the heavens, it's looking at the people around you.

Here's why I consider social activity just as important as physical and mental activity: there's no greater impact on our physical and mental well-being than the in-person social bonds we create throughout our lifetime.

We're social animals. We're wired to pick up social cues from other people. Our sixth sense exists, and it's our social sense. The more neuroscience research that is done, the more we're finding that social wellness is fundamental to our overall well-being.

We now know that seeing other people treated fairly drives the reward center of our brains. We now know that being rejected socially feels just like physical pain. We now know that there are specific "social centers" of our brain that need to be nurtured. Time we spend with other people can have a rejuvenation effect (if they're the right people).

Self-reported loneliness and isolation are at record levels, across all generations, with particular focus on younger generations. This is fascinating to me—you typically hear of the forgotten older generations reporting loneliness. And while everyone seems to have an opinion on the causes of loneliness (technology, among other things), the fact of the matter is that many of us have to work hard to build an in-person social network.

The reason we have to work hard at being social is because making friends is extremely difficult as an adult. We feel more pressure on status than we did as children, we have started down the path of settling into our interests, and we're very quick to find the people we *don't* like instead of the people we do.

Yet we reflect the people closest to us and around us. To have an understanding of your social strategy, you need to ask two questions: Are the people around you making you better? Who is picking *you* to be around to make *them* better?

The book Connected: *How Your Friends' Friends' Friends Affect Everything You Feel, Think, and Do* takes a data-based, analytical view of a person's network (Christakis and Fowler 2011). Where and how you fit within any network of people can dictate many things, such as weight gain and employment.

When we speak about our network, we generally think about it in a work context. But as the world evolves, and the economy changes, your network is ever more reliant on personal connections. We don't have the capacity to keep a "work group" and a "home group." And even if we did, why bother?

And while some of you claim introversion over extroversion, it's still relatable to you. Your social needs are still a requirement, albeit in different ways. Introversion is not an aversion to spending time with people, it's an aversion to spending *too much* time with people. People with introversion (like myself) tend to recharge by themselves and get their energy from reflection and quiet time. Others may get their energy from being in crowds of people. Regardless of where you fall, each of us needs to connect with the outside world in our specific way.

We have emotional connections to the families and friends that have been with us through good and difficult times. Our extended network is massive, with thousands of people just a few degrees away. Over many years we have met many people, and each of these people hold a place in our lives. What we do with these people is up to us.

Like the other chapters, there are three areas of social preparation for the new economy, each with very specific roles and services. First, we have a support system, which is what we think of when we think of a social network. Second, we have micro-interactions, such as with a bus driver or barista. And third, an area I call newbies: a need to meet new people. Let's jump right in.

Support System

First and foremost, everybody needs a support system. This support system doesn't have to look like anything in particular—it's yours. It could be family, friends, business associates, and the like. When things get rough, or if we need an ear to bend, that support system will keep us going.

Building your support system isn't necessarily easy, however. We automatically think of today and the people around us. But if you aren't where you need to be today, you must ask yourself some difficult questions: Have you built the proper support system? Are the people that are around you going to help you get to where you need to go? I guarantee that there's at least one person in your world who's pulling you back.

Relationships are difficult, and I'm not just talking about marriage. All relationships. As we get older, these relationships build banks that come with twenty, thirty, forty years of history, context, and challenges. For example, when I work with family businesses, most of the arguments and frustrations aren't from the business world but things that happened when people were teenagers. One person asks, "Why didn't this invoice go out?" and the family member responds, "Well, when you were eighteen, you broke my favorite vase!"

It's the same with a business network or a personal sphere. History and context dictate where you're going to go. If you surround yourself with highly successful people, your chances of success are significantly increased. It's like the *Moneyball* example—we must be focused on increasing our chances of scoring a run; however, much of that comes from the people who bat before us.

In the first *Rocky* movie, Rocky said it well: "You hang out with nice people, you get nice friends, y'understand? You hang out with smart people, you get smart friends. You hang out with yo-yo people, you get yo-yo friends! Y'see, it's simple mathematics." Simple mathematics. You're a reflection of who you surround yourself with.

Of course, it's never that easy. Nobody will just give you their time and not expect anything in return. So, while one aspect is getting the people around you to be the best possible ones, we have to put ourselves out there so that other people will want to select us. It's like a circle-of-life thing.

Think of it like a bank. In order to pull out some money (gain value from someone), you have to deposit money (provide value), or at least have good credit (reputation). No reputation and no deposit? No money.

I see it often with networking groups. As the year comes to a close, many people who have sales deadlines start networking aggressively because they have to hit their targets. They're nowhere to be seen early in the year, but they come around when they need something. Sometimes they get what they need, but often they don't. I'm not signing a new contract with someone I just met.

The same goes for job hunters. Many people come networking when they're looking for a job, but never before. It's backwards. When you need a job, you're already too late. Building relationships now, while you're employed, and less stressed and less desperate, allows you to build equity for when you need a favor. Your next good job isn't going to come from sending out resumes or filling out online applications. Your next good job comes from someone in your network who makes an introduction. That introduction opens the door, gives reputation credit, and allows you to take out that money.

Think through the people who you have around you. They're the ones that are going to help you build whatever dynasty or reputation you wish to have. They're your PR people, your champions, the coach in the corner of the boxing ring shouting to get up off the mat. You can find those people, but you have to be their coach as well.

Micro-interactions

Micro-interactions are interesting. We practically never think of them, yet they're a necessary part of our environment. They have as significant an impact as your support system but in a completely different way: they're purely surface oriented. The purpose of your micro-interactions is to remind you that you're part of something bigger.

A micro-interaction is exactly what it sounds like: It's the interaction with the barista when you get your coffee. It's the "Have a nice day" from the librarian or the "Thanks for riding" from the bus driver. It's the weird face and head nod we make to someone else waiting for the elevator with us. We've countless interactions daily with strangers and acquaintances, and that provides psychological value.

Having a diverse balance of both a support system (strong ties in our network) and micro-interactions (weak ties in our network) provides both physical and mental health benefits. Research is ongoing; however, studies are beginning to link different types of social time to lower levels of depression and anxiety.

Here's why: a support system may not be with you all the time, but your micro-interactions are. Your support system could be thousands of miles away; those people who have deep relationships with you and who you go to with your challenges or for understanding. Your micro-interactions are all around and can be used when you need them. A trip to the coffee shop or the grocery store gives an opportunity for social interaction, at any time, and gives that sense of community and a bigger picture.

Granted, sometimes micro-interactions make you want to punch someone in the face. I won't deny that there are a lot of people out there whose selfishness and ignorance will make your jaw drop. Like the angry lady trying to return a half-eaten donut or the guy standing in front of you in line for fifteen minutes at a fast food restaurant and doesn't know what he wants when he gets to the counter. Frustrations can be found everywhere—but as a rule, the micro-interactions we have are truly beneficial for us.

When I decided to leave the corporate world and start my business, I worked from home. I had a harsh reality hit me: the corporate world didn't just pay me money, it also gave me social interactions. I lost all the small interactions I had on the commute, in the kitchen, at the elevator, in the hallway going to meetings.

It was one of my biggest challenges and completely unforeseen. My mood and my work changed. I found it difficult to focus. I found I was getting more distracted with absolutely zero people around. I discovered that being around other people helped to balance me.

My solution was simple: I would work for part of the day out of a coffee shop or the library. I added more networking meetings into my calendar. I eventually signed up for a coworking space in the city to keep me balanced. Now, I work from home for two or three days a week, but the other days are with other people. My thinking ability and my productivity increased exponentially. What I thought of as "wasting time" on commuting to the city actually had tangible benefits other than time; on days I commuted, I found that the time I spent working was more productive.

I like to call this finding your *Cheers*. I always wanted to find a place where everyone knew my name. Knowing your name and being in a bar are both secondary; the real value of the bar Cheers is that all of the people who went in there had good conversation and were welcomed, not just Norm and Cliff. Even without sharing your name, you were part of the club. And this can happen for you in a bar or on a train, in a diner, or at the park. Increasing your small interactions with other people and remembering that there's something bigger than our small challenges, is a perspective needed as we look at the new economy.

Newbies

Changing perspective brings you to the third part of your social world: newbies. One of the most important aspects of mental wellness is embracing the idea that you might be wrong; and there's no better place and time to discover your false beliefs than when you meet new people.

Meeting new people and gaining new perspectives aligns perfectly with your belief system. It flexes your belief system, makes you question your assumptions, and (hopefully) gives you a greater understanding of yourself. It challenges us to be open-minded and to see how other people think and feel differently, that their experiences have built a person who doesn't see things the same way we do.

As we build our social networks, we gravitate towards people who think like us, such as in politics, on religion, and about sports. While this has its benefits, it also has its dangers. We risk living in an echo chamber; assumptions become beliefs, story becomes gospel, and an us-versus-them mentality can emerge.

It challenges us to be open-minded. It challenges us to have basic social skills and manners. It challenges us to recognize that there are people out there who aren't like us. And that's a good thing. You don't have to agree with everything another person says, but you do need to show him or her respect for not having the same opinion as you.

Part 3 "Be Teachable" will have more on developing a *curiosity mindset*, but it needs to be said that meeting new people, in a truly effective and beneficial way, requires us to be interested and respectful of their views. I typically don't engage in political or religious (or sports) discussions, simply because the topics can be so divisive that judgment can cloud perspective. That said, developing relationships to the point where good, curious conversations on those topics can be had with a person of an opposing view is a great goal to move towards.

Meeting with new people and acknowledging different perspectives can be daunting. After all, it's difficult to make new friends or meet new people as an adult. We bring our baggage, our perceived status, some ridiculous "elevator pitch" that we've worked on so that we can present and enhance a "personal brand" that everyone will love and we'll rock it. It's difficult to meet new people because we put too much pressure on ourselves to do it.

One of the biggest complaints I hear from people is how much they hate networking. Without a doubt, this lack of desire needs to be overcome—it's fundamental to surviving in the new economy. But the big secret about networking events and meeting new people is that it gets significantly easier the more you do it.

We don't like meeting new people because the pressure is too intense. We work ourselves up to ensure that we're presenting ourselves in the best possible way. We walk into a room and feel like there's a spotlight on us, and our entire time we're focused on "us" and what we're doing instead of the people we're supposed to be meeting. That's backwards.

The *spotlight effect* is a well-known psychological phenomenon wherein people believe that they're being observed much more closely than they are. For example, you might have a small stain on your shirt or a small zit on your neck and you feel like everyone is staring at it. In reality, nobody notices.

One of the other secrets about networking is that everyone is thinking about themselves also and has the same anxiety you do about meeting new people, so no one is going to notice any of the little things about you.

To stave this effect, we should enter into a networking event or a meeting with a new person completely focused on *them*. Here's why: we want people to remember us. And we do that by making people feel good. there's no better way to make someone else feel good than by being interested in what they have to say.

We remember subtle emotions, not facts in an elevator speech. By being curious about the person in front of you (and, by the way, taking the pressure off them by giving them someone to speak with at an event), they'll remember you as a person who noticed them and gave them time in a meaningful way. Also, if you can find something that they enjoy speaking about, the conversation will just flow from there.

It took me many years to learn how to network and go to an event. Oftentimes, I would show up, walk around the room, and leave without speaking to anyone. Other times, I would force myself to have three conversations, and when they were done, I was out. I was petrified of standing alone, worried what other people would think, and felt the pressure of needing to impress rather than just enjoy the company of the people I was around.

I, fortunately, had a breakthrough. I knew networking was vital to my business, but I wasn't doing enough of it. I started to ask myself why I hated it so much, what was making me so nervous, and what I could change. I came up with two questions.

First, when going into a networking event, I ask myself, "What do I need to do in order to enjoy this conversation/event/etc.?" I frame it into something that I know I'll enjoy, because I know I'm putting my best self forward if I'm having fun. Maybe it's sharing some really interesting news I just received. Maybe it's playing a mental game (how many lawyers will I meet?). Generally, I know now what I enjoy most about networking is recounting the interesting people I met.

The second question I ask myself is this: "Will this person be happy we spoke?" It moves the focus away from me and ensures that I'm being a conversationalist first. My best networking comes when I don't try to sell anything. When the pressure of selling anything comes off, you're free to enjoy the conversation and the company of the people around you. After all, we don't network to sell to the people we're meeting. The purpose of networking is to build a network, creating relationships that can be beneficial later.

Building your social system, having your micro-interactions, and meeting new people is the basic formula for social success. The benefits impact both your physical and your mental self in countless ways and put you on the path to be successful in the new economy.

Chapter 11: Financial Preparation

I would be remiss to not include something on financials when talking about surviving in the new economy. It gets its own section and callout because it's vital. Financial preparation isn't the same as the others because there are more outside influences; it's a puzzle to figure out and ignoring it is done at your own peril.

Money is important. We know this. We also know it won't solve all your problems. But having money solves all your *money problems*, which are typically the biggest problems that people have.

Most of my corporate career was in the financial industry. I didn't provide financial advice, but I had significant exposure to how both money managers and individual investors think about money and how they are misaligned. During my career in finance, I helped create several financial education programs to help people both understand their finances and begin the path to financial independence. What I consistently found was that most people lacked the very basics to just get started. So that's where we'll begin.

Money is a sensitive and uncomfortable subject. We resent not having it, and often find it intimidating to try to put together a plan. Financial planning appears to be complicated and stress inducing, with experts sharing opinions, acronyms galore (ETF, CD, REIT), and countless methods "you should" follow. When we're faced with something that's stress inducing and we don't fully understand it, the easy response is to ignore it until it goes away. But your finances are one area where you need to hit that shit head-on, ask the right questions, and understand what's needed. Fortunately, I have a simple outline to get you started. Because getting started is part one and too many people put it off, it's the most important part.

Saying you can't save for the future because you don't understand mutual funds is a step too far; they're two very different things. Focusing on the stock market when you have more credit card debt than savings is unhelpful. So, let's focus on the three things that you need to answer to begin planning your financial future.

Fundamentally what you need is as follows:

1. You should always be able to articulate your net worth.
2. You should have a budget and understand where your money is going.
3. You should have a target that you want to hit for savings.

Until you have those answers in place, you're blindly throwing money around. Questions about mutual fund fees, advisor fees, or option trading strategies can all have their day in the sun in the future. But until we answer the first three questions, those questions are a distraction.

We have a fear of the unknown, and the unknown is typically what prevents us from acting. I once had a conversation with a friend that went something like this:

> Friend: "I'll never be able to retire."
> Me: "How come?"
> Friend: "I'll never have the money!"

> Me: "How much do you need?"
>
> Friend: "I don't know—but I won't have it."
>
> Me: "Well how far along are you?"
>
> Friend: "No idea. What are you ordering?"

How can we claim to not have enough if we don't know what enough is? And that's the purpose of this exercise: to give us context as to what we're working with. By defining the parameters, we now can create a plan. If your net worth is negative, ignoring it isn't going to make it go away. It's time to start changing that trajectory.

And, to be clear and let you get to work, here is how I define these terms:

For your net worth, add up the value of all your savings, investments, home equity, 401(k) plan, and so on; add everything up with value. Then, subtract all of your obligations, like credit card debt, remaining mortgage balance, auto loans. That sum is your net worth. If it's negative, that's OK: now you know; now you can address it. That net worth is what you have to retire and not work anymore. Is it enough? You don't know until you complete the next two steps.

For your budget, you have to understand where your money is going: rent and mortgage payments, restaurants, booze, coffee shops, internet. There are apps that can help you categorize. You may be surprised at where you're wasting some money.

Finally, your savings goal. Here's the fun trick: take your annual budget (what you spend in a year) and multiply it by twenty-five. That's a quick, down and dirty way to find out how much you'll need to have in savings and investments to retire. According to what you're spending, and a conservative 4 percent return in the market, you'll need to hit that number to keep your current standard of living after working. If that number is ridiculously high, then it's time to start thinking about some changes.

As GI Joe said: "Knowing is half the battle." Those three exercises give you a fountain of information to start making changes, create a plan, and focus on your financial goals. If you have a negative net worth and a savings goal of $12 million, maybe that BMW you were looking at isn't the right decision.

Knowing your numbers also provides value for those who have been saving. You may find that you're already halfway or more to your ultimate savings and investment goals. That helps you make fundamentally different decisions on where you spend your time. If you have hit your net worth goal, you may not wish to stay at a job that is sucking the life out of you. You then have the power and ability to take on different types of work, spending your time in different ways as you move through this experience we call life.

Everyone's how and why are different—it's important to find yours. Some can take their investing to the next level by themselves by doing passive investing and a broad index fund, while others prefer active investing with an advisor. How you get there is your responsibility and choice. But having a base, a foundation, on which you can begin to have the difficult money discussions is essential. Otherwise it will always be an unnerving prospect in the back of your mind. Everything can be accomplished; we just have to know what we're dealing with.

Part Three: Be Teachable

To kindness and wisdom we make promises only; pain we obey.

—Marcel Proust, *A Remembrance of Things Past*

Chapter 12: Learning Pains

There are lessons in pain. We need to experience a lesson for it to take root; for instance, from a young age, we learn not to touch the hot stove by touching the hot stove. So it makes sense that much of the advice we *don't* take is given to us by other people, but the advice we give ourselves, driven by our own experiences, we'll follow time and again. Like most spouses, I experience this often with my wife.

There are different types of pain with different types of lessons. Yes, physical pain is a big one, but humiliation is also pain. Pride can be painful and social rejection is pain. As a matter of fact, our brain treats all pleasure and pain in the same area. Social rejection, like being humiliated or being dumped, is treated the same way in your brain as breaking your arm. It's why we're so scared of doing things like speaking in public: it's a room full of potential social rejection or humiliation, and we want to run from it like a physical threat.

But speaking in public can also be a great rush. Most people I work with on public speaking generally say afterwards, "It wasn't that bad." The way to improve your public speaking is to do it again and again until it gets easier. We're teaching ourselves, through experience (and sometimes pain), that the uncomfortable moments we experience are often the most beneficial for our development.

That's not to say that we should buy a hammer to hit our thumb. But embracing these uncomfortable moments and recognizing that there are lessons in each one makes them significantly easier to take.

We have recognized that massive change is happening (part 1), we're working to prepare ourselves (part 2). Through education and learning, we can evolve and adapt to change in our journey, which means that we have to be teachable if we're going to succeed in the new economy. That requires us to put humility in its place, be curious, and embrace vulnerability.

I wasn't open to that in my corporate career. Generally driven by my own insecurity and by a fear of humiliation as a carryover from my childhood, I entered the building each day in pure judgment mode. I wasn't open to learning or feedback, making me an impossible person to manage.

I wasn't a bad employee; I got my work done and I did it well. But much of my frustration in the corporate world was my place in it: I wasn't developing the way I should and moving up the ladder the way I anticipated because I wouldn't be a *learner*. I wasn't open to asking questions, just providing answers. I couldn't articulate where I wanted to go, and I wasn't open to asking for help.

Much of being teachable is being open to the experience of learning and being comfortable with ourselves. We can't be everything to everyone, we don't need to have all the answers, and we need to give ourselves permission to ask questions.

It doesn't always have to be painful, but it can be uncomfortable. The painful lessons of the past put us in lanes: guidelines that direct where we do and don't want to go. For me, the humiliation I experienced asking questions as a child had a significant influence on my ability to ask questions as I got older. I was often embarrassed to ask questions or my questions were quickly dismissed, and as a protective barrier, I just stopped asking them. It wasn't a good approach or a healthy mindset.

The boundaries of our comfort are constantly evolving, provided we are willing to challenge them. While our comfort has general borders, our growth, happiness, and success all come from slightly pushing those boundaries and getting uncomfortable. Sometimes there will be pain when learning the lesson, but our growth comes when we learn to reflect on the discomfort, identify the valuable nuggets of learning, regroup, and carry on, perhaps with our head held just a centimeter higher.

When we recognize that there's a world larger than us (and that we only have one spin on this planet), we change our actions and perspective, while allowing opportunities to open themselves in front of us. We can realize that the emotional pain we feared isn't really that bad, and when we reflect on our past, our fears of humiliation or rejection are either unfounded or mostly irrelevant.

The three aspects in this section were my lessons. Learning these lessons and changing my mindset years ago would have saved me significant grief, massively improved my work relationships, and saved me a lot of headaches. But what I learned from those headaches is what I can take forward to avoid those pitfalls in the future.

My philosophy on asking questions has completely changed the way I work and live. Asking more questions, giving myself permission to want something, and welcoming the fact that I could be wrong have been some of the most important changes I've made. The following three chapters cover how you can learn to change too.

Chapter 13: Put Humility in Its Place

> We cannot attribute to fortune or virtue
> that which is achieved without either.
>
> —Machiavelli, *The Prince*

I believe there's a misalignment, or rather clarity needed, on the relationships between humility, curiosity, vulnerability, and success.

Humility is often touted as an important component of both effective leadership and success, and with proper guard rails, it can be—but humility can have its dangers. When we're told and taught to "Be humble," we're effectively being given lazy advice that's easy to bestow on other people; also, the advice is a judgmental sentiment that dictates the way other people should be.

Humility is having or showing a modest or low view of one's own importance. That's not a good thing. Humility, in that definition, will not help you as the economy changes. A line needs to be drawn between recognizing what we're capable of and communicating that proudly versus a humble view of our own importance.

People like to "see humility," but they're really saying, "Don't be an arrogant ass." Humility, confidence, and arrogance are an intertwined ball of subjectivity. We find arrogant people so obnoxious because there's no belief that they're capable of what they're speaking of. Arrogance is an attempt to deflect from some other area, whether an insecurity or something else. But since it's a deflection, not an accurate representation of who that person is, our bullshit meter goes up, marking the deflection as inauthentic, so we push it away.

What we want to see, rather, is *humble confidence*, a recognition that we understand our capability and we commit to following it. But again, confidence is subjective; telling someone to be confident doesn't help anything. It's like telling them to be a leader, to be innovative, to be humble: it's judgmental and provides zero direction whatsoever.

Confidence, in a leadership capacity or otherwise, needs to be individually defined, understood, and developed through a period of discovery. Confidence is a love of and belief in self. A confident person is comfortable in their skin and recognizes their place in the world or is in the process of discovering it. Also, a confident person is comfortable talking about their likes and dislikes with objectivity and recognizing that other people have different views. Confident people are in control.

All these words are used to describe an aspect of personality, and one of our additional challenges is that that personality has two aspects: what we feel internally and what other people see. On the one hand, my set of values, the things I find important, my attributes of self, are all part of my personality. On the other hand, what you see, the words you would use to describe me, are also part of my personality. And those two sets often conflict.

"Feeling confident" and having other people describe you as confident are two very separate things; "feeling humble" and having other people describe you as humble is just as separate. Take a two-pronged approach when working on yourself: (1) internalize certain attributes to discover yourself and then (2) determine how best to show those attributes to other people.

Confidence, however, isn't without self-doubt. Many of the people I speak to about confidence always focus on the occasional doubt they have in the back of their minds. They may be afraid of being discovered as a fraud (imposter syndrome) or of failure (inner saboteur).

But doubt is a good thing: it's an awareness and focus on capability. How you respond to doubt is what matters. Many people talk about doubt as the reason for inaction, but the ironic thing about doubt is that the only way to get rid of it is to act.

When we internalize humility and minimize our accomplishments or importance, it quickly becomes detrimental. This deprecation of capability is designed to keep us in our place and mentally prevents us from trying to achieve more.

We all, hopefully, know the rules of common decency. Manners exist for us to treat people with civility, and acting appropriately is designed to make people feel comfortable around us. *Blast From the Past*, the movie mentioned in the beginning of the book, has one of my favorite lines of any movie: "The simple definition of a lady or a gentleman is someone who always tries to make sure the people around him or her are as comfortable as possible." But over time, because of what we're taught, acting appropriately in the eyes of other people may not be beneficial to us. I'm a perfect example.

For years I had this fantastic ability to not take credit for anything that I did. I had a psychological block, and to this day I still feel very uncomfortable taking compliments. Whether at work, with family, or friends, I never spoke much about what I wanted, I never spoke about what excited me. I let my years of being told to be humble affect me; as a result, I wouldn't let myself want something or be proud of an accomplishment. Bragging was a four-letter word in our house.

The problem with this thinking, especially now in the new economy, is that if you don't dictate what you want and take ownership of what you've accomplished, somebody else will.

I found that I couldn't communicate things I was proud of—I used to always think, "Will this be seen as arrogant?" Consequently, I would no longer communicate anything that I was looking to do: I deferred. After all, the line between confidence and arrogance is both thin and subjective.

In 2019, I completed my first (and likely last) Ironman. The training and the race were a massive physical and mental undertaking. It was a major accomplishment. I did it. I'm proud of it. And I want the world to know it.

My initial response after finishing it, though, was just to say, "Oh, you know, it's nothing. I'm just grateful to have done it." Meanwhile, inside, I'm thinking, "You better fucking believe I did an Ironman! I worked hard for it, and I'm excited to say that I accomplished something I set out to do! Ask me anything about it. I love talking about it."

But the old humble Jim can't say that. I tiptoed along the line of pride and arrogance. I felt that by talking about what I wanted, and what I accomplished, was to be seen as bragging. But why can't we be proud of the things we set out to achieve? Why can't we talk about the challenges we are setting out for ourselves? It's by talking about what we're looking to do and accomplish, we receive the support we need from the people around us.

When I first signed up to do the Ironman, I told a few people, and within a few days, I was having conversations with strangers who had completed numerous races. My network, the people closest to me, offered up their friends who were able to give advice. I wouldn't have finished the race without talking to them. By stating that I wanted to do it, my network pulled together and got me in front of who I needed to be in front of to accomplish something I wanted to accomplish.

I recognize it was just a race, but the lesson in humility goes beyond that. By articulating your desire to start a new business, your network will move into action. By articulating your desire to find a new job, to build a new hobby, or to take on any particular challenge will bring additional support your way. What we have to do is move beyond the block of humility and embrace the fact that we all want to do something and accomplish things, and we should be proud as hell when we do.

Our humility blocks have multiple levels of difficulty. Externally, we don't want to be perceived as being braggadocious because the perception has a negative connotation, so we worry that "if people perceive me as arrogant, they won't like me. They will talk about me behind my back. What will the neighbors say!"

But also, internally, I was protecting myself. If I didn't get excited for something, or if I didn't ask for anything, I couldn't be rejected or humiliated. It goes back to vulnerability and confidence issues we mentioned in the previous sections.

There's a difference, though, between confidence and arrogance. A wise friend of mine once told me that the difference between confidence and arrogance is follow-through. And when we follow through, appropriately taking credit for our success and giving credit where it's due will only benefit us. Like Machiavelli said, we cannot attribute our success to our hard work if it's because we were given something; however, we can and should credit ourselves with success that we worked hard for.

Appropriate humility begins and ends with the recognition that you don't know everything and that you're part of a much bigger picture. Are you insignificant in the grand scheme of things? Of course. But you're also the most important person—the most significant thing in the world to yourself. You're a learner, and as you get older, despite knowing more, you need to pay attention and continue to learn more.

In high school, I participated in competitive public speaking (read: stud muffin), otherwise known as forensics (not just dead people.) Despite having a bit of talent at both, I didn't have the confidence to try out for the baseball or basketball team, intimidated as a freshman in a new school with an abject fear of failure. As my mother required participation in some kind of extracurricular activity, and with her "suggestion," I joined the forensics team.

It may have been the most important decision I made for a number of reasons. My high school had the premier public speaking team in the nation. We traveled the country, competing against schools in a variety of public speaking categories. We learned how to structure a speech and deliver it with confidence. But, most importantly, we had Tony Figliola.

Tony was our coach, and he had a special understanding of what it took to win. Outside of being one of the top speaking coaches in the world, he also knew a secret: oftentimes you win a competition before you actually compete. Your presence, the way you enter a room, how you carry yourself, all impact the way that other people perceive you. Talent will only get you so far; your presence—that subtle confidence in your capability—will put you over the top.

He reminded us before each tournament: "You are always being watched, by other competitors, by judges, by teachers." Everyone had to wear a suit and dress appropriately, even those who weren't competing. Everyone on the team was required to carry themselves in the most appropriate way—a tall order for high school students. But it worked: people knew that you were on Tony's team just by looking at you.

Yes, we worked hard to win, practicing hours on end. But we won. And I remember the confidence of walking into a room and knowing that I was going to win. Yes, I was nervous, my leg would shake while speaking, but I did what I had to do to let people see a confident speaker. I knew I was ready and that I did the work. I was focused on me and what I was capable of in that moment. Doing so let me win a national championship. I was the top high school public speaker in the country in 1995 (read again: stud muffin).

The lesson is evergreen, and I find myself sharing it with clients all the time. I worked my ass off to practice my speech, from words on the page to hand gestures and emphasis. I did my best to carry myself appropriately, and I was able to focus and hide my nervousness when it mattered. It's the same with operating in the workplace.

When you take your business in front of investors for funding, the decision to give you money is made before you make the request. When you go on a sales call or into a networking event, people decide if they're going to want to do business with you in an instant. Like Malcolm Gladwell (2007) describes in his book *Blink*, people make decisions about us in the blink of an eye.

That's why it's important to control and define who you are as an individual and why it's important to articulate what it is that you want and to align it to your value set. By claiming what you're capable of and unabashedly going after it, you're able to elevate yourself to where you want to be. It's much easier said than done, but putting humility in its place is a necessity for the new economy.

CHAPTER 14: BE CURIOUS

To learn is not to know; there are the
learners and the learned. Memory
makes the one, philosophy the other.

—Alexandre Dumas, *The Count of
Monte Cristo*

I have a theory. I have a belief that the reason
children are so happy, and adults are so miserable,
is because children are curious and learning. When
we're children, everything is new. We have a sense
of awe and wonder; we're making connections we
didn't know existed and regularly get that "Aha!"
moment when we learn something new. It's exciting
to learn.

Fast forward to adulthood where the learning has stopped. We're expected to be the experts, to have the answers, not asking questions. After decades of similar experiences, we bring in judgments and shortcuts. Our years of learning ended with college; now it's time to prove to the world what we know. And while I have always had a desire to be the expert, I've found it's much less fun to just "know," illuminating others but never yourself.

It doesn't have to be that way. This desire to be an expert, to have the answers, is a protective barrier over our own ignorance. The barrier is protection against the humiliation of being wrong—a reflection of our insecurities. We all have times where we feel like impostors; consequently, we don't want others to realize it.

But if you watch a true expert operate, they're full of questions before they come up with answers. From neuroscientists to mechanics, experts can identify patterns but are always open to the possibility that there's something new going on. They have a desire to learn about a specific situation and then to apply that specific situation to research and other information that's available.

The brain likes to take shortcuts. It's designed to operate in the most efficient manner possible. We don't think about the steps to brush our teeth in the morning: we just do them. It's the same with assumptions and judgements we make at the office, at home, and in our community. It's the reason political, religious, and sports discussions always end in disaster: each side "knows" what the other is thinking and responds accordingly. In actuality, eliminating those assumptions and asking questions by fostering a curiosity mindset would make those conversations more productive.

I love asking people how they define the word *question*. Most people have a general idea, but stop at fully defining it. I define a question as a request for information where you legitimately do not know the answer.

What we typically call questions are actually statements in question form. Think about your time in the office—many of the "questions" aren't to solicit information but to send a message or verify a belief. Rhetorical questions and massive assumptions limit knowledge and learning and squash effective and productive conversation.

It's the emotion versus logic conundrum. We often mistake our feelings and emotions for facts and truth. But just because we want something to be true doesn't make it so; also, just because we feel like it should be true also doesn't make it so.

Much of the leadership coaching I'm asked to conduct in an organization is to drive something called *psychological safety*. In a few words, psychological safety is where a person can present an idea, a thought, or a challenge without fear of repercussion or humiliation.

It's so simple, but a novel idea for many organizations. Managers and leadership are pressured and taught to "have the answers," and when an uncomfortable situation arises, they have a natural inclination to squash it. It takes skill and talent to handle the difficult questions and perspectives of so many unique individuals in one place, on one team, all firing at you during a thirty-minute discussion.

That skill, though, is exactly what everyone is looking for in an office, and it has impacts on everything from productivity to culture to revenue. Research shows that the more diverse the company, the better it performs. McKinsey had

186

a study that showed racially diverse companies outperform industry norms by 35 percent (Hunt, Layton, and Prince 2015). The reason why a diverse workforce is so beneficial is because of the cognitive diversity that the people bring. People from different ages, genders, and races all have wildly different experiences. Being able to draw on these perspectives and having everyone recognize that they've something to learn from these views elevates a workplace to an entirely different level.

Having a diverse workforce, by any demographic measure (age, gender, race, etc.), is irrelevant if all people aren't encouraged and welcomed to share their thoughts and experiences. The economic value of a diverse workforce is diminished when we don't allow people to speak up in their natural and productive way. Not being able to share a perspective doesn't just hurt the person who owns it but it hurts the people around them as well. This is a principle that can and should move beyond the office.

Ask yourself the question, Are you the type of person where anyone, regardless of religious, political, or personal belief, can feel comfortable sharing their opinions without fear of dismissal or immediate rebuttal? Extremely few people are, and you need to explore the possibility that you aren't one of them. I do my best to be one of those people, and I know I still have a lot of work to do.

Curiosity, psychological safety, and effective questioning require a separation of logic and emotion. When we align our belief system to our questions and feel the need to defend ourselves in our questions, we aren't actually being curious. Rather, we're using our questions to be proven correct. But opening ourselves to share in another individual's perspective broadens our horizon significantly. These new experiences lay influence on our own perspective and improve our ability to make decisions down the road.

This improved decision-making capability and learning mindset also has significant positive effects on our stress levels. Our body operates in one of two modes at all times: (1) our sympathetic, or fight-or-flight, nervous system or (2) our parasympathetic, or rest-and-relaxation, nervous system. When one is working, the other isn't, and we necessarily need to go back and forth between the two. Stress makes us take action, and de-escalation of stress lets us catch our breath. We need both.

Our ability to learn new things is driven by our parasympathetic nervous system. Our desire to be open to new ideas and to take them in, comes from lower stress levels. For example, when we travel to another culture on holiday, most of us are polite. We're curious about a different culture and learning new things. We're relaxed, we're learning, and we're happy. It's vacation, after all.

Fast forward to coming home: we're suddenly barking coffee orders at the barista, shouting in traffic, and complaining about Greg in the legal department. We aren't interested in new ideas or new learning; we're using our stress levels to "get things done" and "off of our plate."

The irony is that more things get finished when we bring that curiosity and learning mindset to the office. By engaging in discussion, by asking legitimate questions, we have individuals build their own accountability and understanding of what's expected and what can get done. Through questions, you'll find that the people around you begin taking on more responsibility because they understand, in their way, what needs to get done.

So, we have to be able to admit that we don't know something to begin cultivating a curiosity mindset, which is a mindset easier to implement when we embrace *vulnerability*.

CHAPTER 15: EMBRACE VULNERABILITY

> The awakening to your own ignorance
> is the beginning of wisdom.
>
> —Frank Crane

Give yourself permission to be wrong.

It's one of my biggest hindrances and one of the easiest areas of growth for most people I work with; however, admitting that you might be wrong or don't know something is one of the most cathartic experiences you can enjoy.

However, holding yourself accountable for something can be painful. It can provide feelings of humiliation, insignificance, and failure. But these are internal feelings, which means that they can't be seen by others and that you can affect them. As there are lessons in pain, lessons in vulnerability are to be addressed, learned, and embraced.

In the previous chapter, we talked about asking questions, and how, since we don't have all the answers, we need to ask the right questions to get where we want to go. Not having the answers is one thing but being wrong is something else entirely, and going through the process of recognizing when we're mistaken and being open to the fact that we can change our perspectives, ideas, and beliefs is a life-changing prospect.

Vulnerability is swiftly becoming one of the new corporate words out there that people strive for. I call it "the new humility." What used to be considered a weakness is now preached as one of the fundamental aspects of effective leadership.

But like many of the words we use in this book, it needs defining. Vulnerability is a massive concept. In one sense, it *could* mean a weakness or danger. But when we talk about vulnerability for surviving in the new economy, we're talking about vulnerability that holds hands with accountability—that is, a vulnerability that recognizes that I can be wrong most of the time, that I don't have the answers, and that I can use the help of other people. It's ultimately a re-evaluation of your expectations and a recognition that you can act without guarantees of success. It's an embracing of who you are even if you don't agree with something. It's a learning tool and mindset to help you relate to others, solve problems, and become a productive leader.

A quick note on what vulnerability *isn't*: vulnerability isn't about sharing everything. The details of your divorce, the crazy things you did over the weekend, or the hard-core emotional feelings you're having in the moment. Those may be fine for some people, but not most. That's not the type of vulnerability we're talking about. It's not about oversharing feelings, challenges, or problems, it's about being in tune with who you are, being curious, and being open to the fact that you have something to learn from every person you meet.

With pain comes stress. And in times of stress, like the massive change occurring in the world around us, we put up invisible protective barriers. In this period of change, we don't want to be perceived as unknowledgeable, ineffective, or wrong. We have a desire to be seen as an expert and to be considered an essential part of any group or organization.

But the essential members of any group or organization are those that ask questions, partner with other people, and create plans together. By including other people in a learning and discovery process, they'll feel that you're essential—and feelings drive most of our decisions.

When we're stressed and we're trying to showcase our expertise, we tend to put down other ideas. When things feel out of control, we have this subconscious response to try to appear "above" everything else, to be superior to other people. We all do it. And in our attempt to elevate ourselves over everything, we can't learn.

Think about meetings you take part in at the office; every meeting has one of these people: the person who speaks up only to tell you why something won't work. It's a stress response. Instantly putting down new ideas, rather than asking questions on how it could work, is an effort to show that we're superior, or smarter, than what's being presented. It's an invisible barrier to productivity, and it's divisive. Stressful times, ironically, lead to less collaboration; however, sharing that stress makes it easier to bear.

The effective leaders, rather, ask questions. They request information, knowledge, and expertise from the people around them. Everyone has lanes in which they're successful and knowledgeable, so allowing people to showcase those lanes makes them want to be around you.

The curiosity and vulnerability attributes I write about will change the entire culture of a household, community, or organization. It's about cultivating a desire to learn from each other, regardless of expertise. Parents can learn from children, and senior executives from entry-level employees. Creating an environment around you to encourage learning, to welcome new ideas, to allow people to share what they believe without fear of humiliation will separate you from others in the new economy.

This openness—also known as psychological safety—is fundamental to bringing out the best in the people around you. Psychological safety goes back to the premise of this book: to deal with change around you, focus on yourself. Like I wrote in part 2, "Be Prepared," by focusing on you, you can serve other people. It's time again to ask the question: Are you doing your best to make the people around you feel welcome and of value?

Humility, curiosity, and vulnerability are all valuable in their specific ways, but the two we should be focusing on are curiosity and vulnerability: curiosity is an interest in other people, while vulnerability is a focus on the self.

In a self-serving, full-circle kind of way, we focus on improving ourselves so that we can improve the people around us. When we improve the people around us, and they feel that they have improved because of you, they'll be your ally and assist you with whatever it is that you need. By then assisting you with what you need, you continue to improve yourself, and so on.

That lovefest of a circle is precisely what will generate success in the new economy. It's basic old-school, interpersonal-relationship stuff—but sometimes we need to go back to the basics. We'll especially see that in our next part, which is about finding your wisdom.

Part Four: Be Wise

Upgrade your gray matter . . . because
one day it may matter . . .

—Deltron 3030

My personal manifesto includes eight points and
two quotations:

I am Jim Frawley, and from this day forward, I
will be the ideal version of myself. The first step in
helping other people is to be an example for them.

The cardinal virtues are my drivers: prudence,
temperance, fortitude, and justice.

The ideal Jim is fit and healthy. He is a nondrinker,
a nonsmoker, and a healthy eater. Everything
that goes into me will help me become a physical
representation of who I am. People will look at me
and know what capability means.

I am a learner. Education is in everything, and I will find joy in the simplicity of life and the variety of other people.

I am motivated. I will work harder and smarter than anyone else. And I will teach other people to be the same. When I can't find work immediately, I will create it.

—Michel de Montaigne: "The most outstanding gifts are destroyed by idleness."

I will never force my help on anyone. The only person I need to prove anything to is myself.

Everything I do is for me, to be the best person I can be, and that will show, without words, what other people can be.

—Marcus Aurelius: "Waste no more time arguing what a man should be. Be one."

I am now the person I dream of being. There's no dress rehearsal for a wonderful life.

In 1979 Michael Jackson wrote what CBS News called a "manifesto." It was a short note that Michael wrote to himself, defining the entire persona he wanted to create. Growing up part of the Jackson

5, he wanted to shed the image of being the cute kid in a family band and go out on his own, build a new character, and become the ultimate global sensation. He committed to working harder than anyone else before him. He wanted, in his words, to become "magic" and better than all the others wrapped into one. He wrote:

> MJ will be my new name—no more Michael Jackson. I want a whole new character, a whole new look. I should be a totally different person. People should never think of me as the kid who sang "ABC," [or] "I Want You Back." I should be a new, incredible actor/singer/dancer that will shock the world. I will do no interviews. I will be magic. I will be a perfectionist, a researcher, a trainer, a master. I will be better than every great actor roped into one. I 'must' have the most incredible training system—to dig and dig and dig. I will study and look back on the whole world of entertainment and perfect it; take it steps further from where the greatest left off. (*CBS News* 2013)

Say what you want about Michael Jackson and his controversial life, but you can't deny that he did it. In the history of global entertainment, there are few people who were as big or adored as Michael Jackson. He took a desire to "shock the world," personified it, created it, and became it.

I was never a big fan of Michael Jackson, but when I heard about the manifesto, I googled it. It amazed me that someone could completely change a persona based on a few sentences. Each one of his sentences had meaning and direction for him. As I struggled with defining who and where I wanted to be in the new economy, I did the same.

As I've mentioned throughout this book, success in the new economy requires a focus inward, an understanding of yourself and your values. It also requires an understanding of who you wish to be. They go hand in hand, and oftentimes we speak of this understanding as a means to an end, to help us find our "dream job" or what we want to do in our spare time. But I would argue the ongoing investigation of self, the constant unwrapping of emotion, desire, and frustration, *is* the actual end. Our constant inner investigation gives us context as we learn new things and provides parameters as we develop what's truly necessary to be successful: *wisdom*.

The new economy isn't just about planning and making goals—though those are always good— it's about decision-making as well. With the world moving so fast around us, the time has come to learn to make good, swift, and effective choices, and we make good choices, the best choices for us, when we understand who we are and what we need.

With uncertainty comes stress, and much of our satisfaction and vision of success comes from *stress mitigation*; for example, having money eliminates the stress of needing money. Much of the stress we deal with today is surrounded by whether we're making the right decisions. When we're sure of ourselves, when we have figured out our value set and our levers, we're able to mitigate that level of stress to focus on more important things.

My hesitation to make decisions before was grounded in whether I could defend my decisions to someone else. But, by creating my parameters, by defining my manifesto, the need to defend my decision to someone else becomes irrelevant because I know that I'm making the best decisions for me.

More times than not, a good decision today is better than a perfect decision made too late. As the world passes us by, we need to remember that there's very little that we can't "undo." Most decisions we make are fairly inconsequential; when we start down one particular path, we'll quickly know if it's right or wrong for us.

When I was launching my business, I found I was getting stuck with creating my website. There were so many decisions to make: small, tiny decisions that just piled up into a mess, halting productivity and causing frustration. I also wanted to start a podcast, but I wasn't sure if I should, could, would.

Both solved themselves on the same day. In speaking to a cousin, who builds web sites, I learned that it didn't matter what decisions I made for the site or what I spoke about on the podcast, because I could always change it. The important thing was to decide a path and begin doing it.

In most decisions you make, you can undo them. Don't like the food you cooked? You can order a slice of pizza. Don't like your website template for your business? Change it. Or, sometimes it's more severe but the principle is the same: Don't like the new job or your new spouse? You can find a new one. We spend so much time worrying about what the right, perfect decision is that we end up delaying everything over something inconsequential.

Okay, hang on. If you're looking for a new spouse, *at least* try to open the conversation and see what's not working—I'm not completely heartless. I can't describe leaving a spouse as inconsequential, of course. But the underlying principle of choice, the notion that *you* can make significant change, is one that should be a driving force behind much of your thinking. A wise perspective recognizes that there's something bigger than whatever decision we're making today.

Wisdom is the ultimate goal, covering everything from your point of view to how you spend your time. Each chapter in this book has a wisdom component, whether from physical or mental preparation and right on through vulnerability and humility. Wisdom is your perspective and the ability to change it. We only have one spin on this little grain of sand we call earth—through wisdom you can make the most of it.

As things change so quickly, we need to create a filter. Mountains of information are created every day; it's too much to take in. As the economy changes, as the workplace changes, as communities and society change, our decision-making turns to what's important: developing the filter for how to focus attention, energy, and time.

The consulting and coaching work I do for organizations centers around people. I make people better, in whatever form that may take: productivity, engagement, interpersonal relationships, and the like. We all have blind spots, so I help people find theirs. This work is predicated on building filters, filters that are important for either the company or the person. Companies keep massive amounts of data on their people. It's not enough to know what to focus on, we need to know what to ignore as well.

Each of us, individually, just like my consulting work, deal with data all day long. We're inundated with data. Statistics and opinions infiltrate our social media feeds, and news media has all the information you need for the day. We're constantly being sold to, so we're constantly given reasons why we need to buy this product or that idea.

Change, in effect, is more data to be analyzed and categorized.

But for corporations and individuals alike, data has a process and a filter it has to go through. We need to take massive amounts of data, cut the fat, and see what's left: that's relevant information. We then have to take the information we have received and, from there, turn that into knowledge. Once we know something, we then have to elevate that into one higher level: wisdom.

This is known as the DIKW pyramid (data, information, knowledge, and wisdom). Its origin is unclear, but I love it as a guide. I think about it in terms of evolving my thought process and questioning whether I'm getting the data, information, and knowledge I properly need to make good, wise decisions.

Wisdom is the key aspect that is generally left out. With knowledge, we "feel" like we have an answer, so we stop. Finding a bit of knowledge that might align with our narrative gives us reason to not continue. But wisdom is that one step further to get where we need to go. One of my favorite sayings says it best: "Knowledge is knowing that a tomato is a fruit. Wisdom is knowing not to put it in a fruit salad."

We all have a desire for wisdom, and we especially have a desire for wisdom amid change because we want to know how to go forward. In uncomfortable, uncertain times, we look for someone to tell us either it's all going to be okay or at least in which direction to go. We're looking for a thinker, but in actuality, we need to be the thinker that we desire.

I've recently seen a resurgent desire for thinking stoically, especially in the business world. Quotes from Marcus Aurelius, Epicurus, Epictetus, and Seneca fly across my desk or are offered up in workshops. I even have one from Marcus Aurelius in my manifesto at the beginning of the chapter.

The Stoics were ancient Greek thinkers and philosophers of ethics curious about how we interact with the world. Behind this resurgence of interest in their work is a desire for wisdom. It's a reach for a simpler, more basic time and thought process—a request to define what's important across all aspects of our lives. When we talk about digital detox, or going into the mountains to catch our sanity, we are, in effect, looking to participate in thinking like a Stoic.

Thinking like a Stoic isn't a bad thing. I love watching people think and develop a desire to think. Thought, philosophy, curiosity—all of these elements are fundamental to the human condition. Today, we have machines to do the thinking for us, but thinking is a muscle that needs to be exercised, and we need to make the time for it.

Most are familiar with the cardinal virtues of Greek and Stoic thinking: prudence, temperance, justice, and strength. Use these as your guide to develop your thinking and to self-evaluate and self-reflect. From prudence (making good choices) to temperance (restraint and moderation, especially from a financial perspective) to justice (your belief system and compass) to strength (keep on keepin' on), we all can have the guide we desire—we just need to build it.

One of the biggest parts of learning on my journey was the ability to reflect, introspect, and be comfortable with myself. It changed how I decided what was important; it changed my behavior and the way that I responded to situations. I stopped doing things I didn't want to do, and I started doing the things that I did want to do. It started a fire in me that began on April 28, 2009 (my thirtieth birthday), which put me on the path to where I am today: I now recognize that I have control over my decisions, I have control over my emotions and attitude, I have control over the choices that I make. And when I make good choices, I become the best person I can be. And once I was truly comfortable with myself, doing things I wanted to do, all of a sudden, I started attracting other people who I needed around me and who were similar in outlook.

That was the beginning for me. I learned that I wished to surround myself with people who could challenge me but had similar interests or ideas. And, in retrospect, these people who I wish to surround myself with won't waste their time with someone who doesn't have that stuff together.

I was going to end the book following its theme, concluding: "Be You." But that's cheesy. I'll end it here, leaving you to go off and do your thing. At the time I write this, I'm eleven years past my epiphany, and the learning is still going on. There's no end, just difficult, uncomfortable, and incredibly fun discovery. With that discovery, you'll rock the new economy.

References

60 Minutes: Overtime. 2013. "MJ's 'Manifesto,' Penned in 1979." *CBS News.* https://www.cbsnews.com/news/mjs-manifesto-penned-in-1979/.

Bandura, Albert. 1982. "Self-Efficacy Mechanism in Human Agency." *American Psychologist* 37 (2): 122–47. https://doi.org/10.1037/0003-066X.37.2.122.

Barry, John. 2018. "Harry's Masculinity Report, USA 2018." Amazon. https://s3.amazonaws.com/harrys-cdnx-prod/manual/Harry%27s+Masculinity+Report%2C+USA+2018.pdf.

Christakis, Nicholas A., and James H. Fowler. 2011. *Connected: How Your Friends' Friends'*

Friends Affect Everything You Feel, Think, and Do. Boston: Little, Brown & Company.

Dalio, Ray. 2017. *Principles: Life and Work*. New York: Simon & Schuster.

Eyal, Nir. 2013. *Hooked: How to Build Habit-Forming Products*. New York: Portfolio.

Frankl, Victor. 2006. *Man's Search for Meaning*. Boston: Beacon Press.

Fuller, R. Buckminster. 1982. *Critical Path*. New York: St. Martin's Griffin.

Gladwell, Malcom. 2007. *Blink: The Power of Thinking Without Thinking*. New York: Back Bay Books.

Hilbert, Martin, and Priscila Lopez. 2011. "The World's Technological Capacity to Store, Communicate, and Compute Information." *Science Magazine* 332 (6025): 60–65. https://doi.org/10.1126/science.1200970.

Hogan Assessments. n.d. https://www.hoganassessments.com/.

Hunt, Vivian, Dennis Layton, and Sara Prince. n.d. "Why Diversity Matters." Mckinsey. https:// www.mckinsey.com/business-functions/organization/our-insights/why-diversity-matters#.

Hyman, Mark. 2018. *Food: WTF Should I Eat: The No-nonsense Guide to Achieving Optimal Weight and Lifelong Happiness*. London: Yellow Kite.

International Data Corporation (IDC). 2020. "Global Datasphere Report." Global DataSphere. https://www.idc.com/getdoc.jsp?containerId=IDC_P38353.

Kurzweil, Ray. 1999. *The Age of Spiritual Machines*. New York: Viking Press.

Lewis, Michael. 2004. *Moneyball: The Art of Winning an Unfair Game*. New York: W.W. Norton & Company.

Lieberman, Mathew D. 2013. *Social: Why Our Brains are Wired to Connect*. New York: Crown.

Martin, Gerald. 2010. *Gabriel García Márquez: A Life*. New York: Vintage Books.

National Institute of Mental Health. "Suicide." NIH. https://www.nimh.nih.gov/health/statistics /suicide.shtml.

Pratt, Laura A., Debrah J. Brody, Qiuping Gu. 2017. "Antidepressant Use Among Persons Aged 12 and Over: United States, 2011–2014." Centers for Disease Control and Prevention. https://www.cdc.gov/nchs/products/databriefs/db283.htm.

Roberts, David. 2018. "After rising for 100 years, electricity demand is flat. Utilities are freaking out." *Vox*. https://www.vox.com/energy-and-environment/2018/2/27/17052488 / electricity-demand-utilities.

Rousseau, Jean-Jacques. (1782) 1953. *The Confessions*. London: Penguin Classics.

Schaffel, Chaiel. 2018. "No Cash Needed at this Café. Students Pay The Tab With Their Personal Data." *National Public Radio*. https://www.npr.org/sections/thesalt/2018/09/29 /643386327/no-cash-needed-at-this-cafe-students-pay-the-tab-with-their-personal-data?utm_source

=pocket&utm_medium=email&utm_
campaign=pockethits.

Tams, Carsten. 2018. "Why We Need to Rethink Organizational Change Management." *Forbes.* https://www.forbes.com/sites/carstentams/2018/01/26/why-we-need-to-rethink-organizational-change-management/#90787b9e93cc.

Vance, J.D. 2016. *Hillbilly Elegy: A Memoir of a Family and Culture in Crisis.* New York: Harper.

About the Author

Jim Frawley is a Columbia University certified Executive Coach and the founder of Bellwether, a company dedicated to helping organizations and people build resiliency, adapt to change, and thrive in rapidly shifting contexts.

Over his twenty-year career, he has internationally created and implemented corporate training programs, complex marketing and PR plans, business strategy and administrative plans, and organizational redesigns. He has worked with clients in eight countries and thirty-nine states to date.

A few years ago, Jim realized that he had a unique capability in getting people to do things they didn't think they could. After some experimentation on using this capability for good or evil, he decided on the good. (But not before convincing an Irish cousin to swim in the Hudson River.)

He is the host of the Bellwether Hub podcast, a big-time reader, a small-time triathlete, and a full-time husband and father.